American
society today

MANCHESTER
UNIVERSITY PRESS

Politics Today

Series editor: Bill Jones

American society today

Edward Ashbee

Manchester University Press

Manchester and New York

distributed exclusively in the USA by Palgrave

Published by Manchester University Press
Oxford Road, Manchester M13 9NR, UK
and Room 400, 175 Fifth Avenue, New York, NY 10010, USA
www.manchesteruniversitypress.co.uk

Distributed exclusively in the USA by
Palgrave, 175 Fifth Avenue, New York,
NY 10010, USA

Distributed exclusively in Canada by
UBC Press, University of British Columbia, 2029 West Mall,
Vancouver, BC, Canada V6T 1Z2

British Library Cataloguing-in-Publication Data
A catalogue record for this book is available from the British Library

Library of Congress Cataloging-in-Publication Data applied for

ISBN 0 7190 6021 4 *hardback*
     0 7190 6022 2 *paperback*

First published 2002

10 09 08 07 06 05 04 03 02   10 9 8 7 6 5 4 3 2 1

Typeset in Photina
by Servis Filmsetting Ltd, Manchester
Printed in Great Britain
by Biddles Ltd, Guildford and King's Lynn

Contents

Tables

Acknowledgements

I am very grateful to Malcolm Coffin, Martin Durham, Ellie Dwight, Ken Dwight, Ross English and Ian Ralston for their comments on early drafts. They saved me from many pitfalls. My thanks should also be extended to Josephine Bryan who copy-edited the manuscript with dedication, skill and patience. The responsibility for remaining errors of presentation, fact or interpretation lies, of course, with me alone.

Introduction

In Europe, popular representations of the US often fall back upon crude carica-
ture. Although there is admiration for the scale of the country's resources
as well as its technological and economic capabilities, US society and the
American character have won few sympathetic portrayals. Indeed, in Britain,
there has long been a degree of latent hostility to the US that is shared by both
right and left. At particular historical moments, it has become manifest. In the
1980s, against a background shaped by the deployment of American missiles
in Western Europe, Martin Carthy, the celebrated English folk musician, captured some widely shared sentiments. In one of his songs he lampooned the US,
citing its 'stone age finesse', 'neanderthal pride', corrupt self-serving politicians
and instinctive imperialism. A generation of comedy programmes such as
Fawlty Towers depicted Americans as aggressive, loud and impatient. Despite its
wealth and comparative opulence, the US was seen as a land characterised by
unfettered individualism, extremes of wealth and poverty, emotional excess
and cultural emptiness. Furthermore, it was said, much of this was being
exported across the globe. Like a row of dominoes, successive countries were
being subjected to a process of **Americanisation** or **coca-colonisation**.

Some of the cruder representations of the US have subsequently been mod-
ified. Television series such as *Friends* and *Seinfeld* offer more developed and less
unsubtle depictions of American life. There were empathetic responses across
the world to the events of September 11th 2001. Nonetheless, many of the
earlier images have proved resilient and still maintain their hold. This book
attempts to construct a counterweight to these by considering the defining features of contemporary American society in a balanced way. It examines:

- the distinctive character of American society and the ways in which it can
  be considered **exceptional**;
- the nature of the 'American dream', its promise of upward mobility, and the
  nature of the contemporary American economy;
- the characteristics of American individualism;

1

- the extent to which American identity also rests upon attachments to family, neighbourhood and nation;
- the role of ethnicity, race and other social cleavages;
- the differences between the regions and the degree to which the US is – in the words of the Pledge of Allegiance – 'one nation indivisible';
- the September 11th attacks on New York and Washington DC.

Some of the debates that attracted widespread attention during the 1980s and 1990s are considered in particular depth. For much of this period there was a succession of **jeremiads**, each of which foresaw the demise of the American nation and the erosion of the principles upon which it had been constructed. The US economy, it was said, had lost its capacity to generate wealth and inspire the 'American dream'. At the same time, the spirit of American individualism had, seemingly, been displaced by mass conformity or a growing dependency upon government provision. Others asserted that the decline of civic participation and the demise of long-established voluntary organisations eliminated the constraints that had traditionally been imposed upon the individualist ethos. From this perspective, the US was increasingly gripped by **hyperindividualism**. There were also claims, particularly from those associated with the conservative right, that family life had been undermined by moral laxity. For others, the US was being pulled apart – or **Balkanised** – by cultural diversity. A common American identity had given way to a multitude of conflicting identities structured around factors such as race, ethnicity, gender and sexuality.

American society today considers these debates and assesses the different perspectives that have been put forward. It provides an introduction to the US for students taking American Studies, politics and sociology, as well as the general reader.

1

American exceptionalism

Many studies of the US emphasise **American exceptionalism**. They highlight the profound contrasts – in terms of society, culture and politics – between the US and the countries of Europe and Asia. The US, it is said, has 'exhibited radical peculiarities that have made its experience categorically different from that of other modern or modernizing countries' (Frederickson 1995: 588–9).

The word 'exceptional' was first employed as a description by Alexis de Tocqueville, the French observer who visited the US in the 1830s and 1840s (Ramalho de Sousa Santos 1994: 18). The concept was also used by activists in the communist movement during the late 1920s as they sought to reconcile the American experience – and the weakness of socialism in the US – with the defining tenets of Marxist theory. Exceptionalism was later revived during the Cold War years as a rationale for, and explanation of, the role of the US in leading the 'free world'. The US, it was said, had been constructed around values such as democracy, freedom and opportunity. It had a mission to promote these across the globe. Although the nature of US foreign policy became much less certain once the Cold War came to a close, the concept of exceptionalism still has adherents. During the 1990s the subject was considered in both scholarly journals and popular commentaries. As Seymour Martin Lipset records: 'The American difference, the ways in which the United States varies from the rest of the world, is a constant topic of discussion and in recent years, of concern' (Lipset 1997: 17).

However, despite its place in the vocabulary, 'exceptionalism' raises two methodological difficulties. First, it goes beyond notions of difference and implies that all other nations – apart from the US – share certain common features or conditions. As Michael Kammen warns, this is difficult to establish: 'The words "unique" and "exceptional" must be used with extreme caution because both imply the existence of a norm that describes most or all other industrialized nations – a norm from which we alone deviate' (Kammen 1993: 1). Second, although the term 'exceptionalism' is widely used, there is little agreement about the features of American society that should be considered exceptional. Some have stressed domestic considerations. Others have – as noted above – emphasised the character of US foreign policy. The concept has taken a number of forms.

The first settlers

In April 1607 Captain John Smith and just over a hundred other English 'Adventurers' established Jamestown in Virginia. It was the first permanent settlement by Europeans in what was to become US territory. During its formative years the settlement was almost destroyed by malaria, dysentry, internecine disputes and deadly struggles with both natives and nature. By early 1608 only 38 of the original settlers were still alive. However, despite these hardships, other migrants followed in the wake of the Jamestown colonists. In 1620 the 'Pilgrim Fathers' and the 'strangers' who travelled with them landed at the northern tip of Cape Cod. This was the beginning of the Puritan settlement in Massachusetts and paved the way for colonisation across New England. By the mid-eighteenth century the European-American population had established itself along much of the eastern seaboard and its numbers had risen to about 1.5 million.

Some argue that American identity was shaped by the process of interaction between individuals, communities and the physical characteristics of the continent. John Harmon McElroy sees the beginnings of this in the experiences of the earliest colonists. Only twelve of the 105 colonists at the Jamestown settlement were listed as 'labourers' while, in contrast, eighty-one were 'gentlemen' who did not expect to engage in manual work. However, conditions were harsh and there was a struggle to ensure that there was a food supply sufficient to ensure survival. As McElroy records: 'The Jamestown colonists had brought with them from Europe a culture unsuitable to the wilderness . . . This ratio of three to one of gentlemen and gentlemen's servants to workers was at the root of Jamestown's early history of misery and starvation' (McElroy 1999: 39–40).

The survival of the Jamestown settlement and the fate of the early colonisation process depended upon large numbers of colonists being granted a few acres of land. This led to a broader system of land ownership than that found in Europe, and the emergence of an egalitarian culture that valued manual work and afforded opportunities to all.

The melting pot

Despite the bitterness of those who have feared economic displacement or the loss of the cultural heritage, mass immigration and integration of newcomers have often been celebrated as defining features of American society and the basis for the creation of a society that differs markedly from those in the 'Old

World'. As early as 1782 J. Hector St John de Crevecoeur, who settled in the US after serving as a soldier with the French armies, published his experiences in *Letters from an American Farmer*. He asked a celebrated question: 'What, then, is the American, this new man?' His answer asserted that American identity rested upon the abandonment of nationalities, beliefs and attitudes that had formerly been held, and the embrace by immigrants of entirely new cultural forms. American character, he argued, rested on:

> ... that strange mixture of blood, which you will find in no other country. I could point out to you a family whose grandfather was an Englishman, whose wife was Dutch, whose son married a French woman, and whose present four sons have now four wives of different nations. He is an American, who, leaving behind him all his ancient prejudices and manners, receives new ones from the new mode of life he has embraced, the new government he obeys, and the new rank he holds ... Here individuals are melted into a great new race of men, whose labours and posterity will one day cause great changes in the world. (Quoted in Gleason 1980: 31)

In the years after Crevecoeur described the American in these terms, the scale of immigration to the US increased dramatically. During the 1830s and 1840s large numbers left Ireland, Germany and the countries of Scandinavia. Towards the end of the nineteenth century there was a shift in the character of the process and, increasingly, migrants were drawn from Southern and Eastern Europe. Against this background, the US continued to represent itself as a new beginning, but also a refuge for those denied freedom and opportunity in the 'Old World'. These feelings were captured in the words of Emma Lazarus, which were to be inscribed on the Statue of Liberty:

> Give me your tired, your poor
> Your huddled masses yearning to breathe free
> The wretched refuse of your teeming shore
> Send these, the homeless, tempest-tost to me:
> I lift my lamp beside the golden door.

> (Quoted in Wright 2000: 290)

Such sentiments were built upon as the notion of the US as a 'melting pot' – a phrase drawn from the title of a 1908 play by Israel Zangwill – gained currency. Zangwill offered a profoundly optimistic vision of the American future and the country's capacity to assimilate immigrants. Everyone could be remade in the American image. In the play, David Quixano, a Jewish émigré from Tsarist Russia, put the concept in visionary terms: 'America is God's Crucible, the great Melting Pot where all the races of Europe are melting and reforming! . . . German and Frenchman, Irishman and Englishman, Jews and Russians – into the Crucible with you all! God is making the American' (quoted in Glazer and Moynihan 1967: 289).

However, although the 'melting pot' is a popularly accepted phrase, it has been subject to sustained criticism as a metaphorical representation of the American experience. Some observers have asserted that the concept of the melting pot obscured the harsher realities of the Americanisation process because it implies that the nationalities and races came together on broadly egalitarian terms. However, in practice, there was a process of assimilation or 'Americanisation'. Immigrants had to accept a culture shaped by British settlers and their descendants. In place of the melting pot, they were subject to 'Anglo-conformity'. As Benjamin Schwarz notes:

> 'Americanization' was a process of coercive conformity . . . various nationalities were made into Americans as ore is refined into gold. 'Americanization' purified them, eliminating the dross. The Americanization movement's 'melting pot' pageants, inspired by Israel Zangwill's play by that name, celebrated conformity to a narrow conception of American nationality by depicting strangely attired foreigners stepping into a huge pot and emerging as clean, well-spoken, well-attired, 'American-looking' Americans, that is, Anglo-Americans. (Schwarz 1998: 72)

Immigrants were taught values derived from British-American traditions. Teaching in the public schools eroded earlier notions of identity and any established cultural attachments. There were night classes for adult immigrants that concentrated on English and civics. Following the outbreak of the First World War, and in its aftermath, there was a systematic campaign for '100 per cent Americanism' which was directed against those who were suspected of maintaining former national loyalties.

In addition, some ethnic and racial groupings were excluded. In particular, the concept of the melting pot was limited to European immigrants. It did not incorporate those who had been brought to the Americas as slaves or migrants from the countries of Asia. At the time notions of the melting pot were being popularised, segregation laws – confining African-Americans to separate and invariably unequal facilities – were being imposed across the southern states. Similarly, Chinese and Japanese-Americans, many of whom had settled in California, faced discriminatory laws and were denied citizenship.

Despite the widespread use of the term to describe the defining characteristics of American society, the process of 'melting' has also in some instances been partial. Some groups deliberately sought isolation. Religious communities such as Mennonites, the old-order Amish and Hutterites sought to build separate communities structured around their own beliefs and **folkways**. Similarly, orthodox Jewish communities, most notably the Lubavitcher Hasidim, maintained distinctive communities in, for example, Brooklyn.

The melting pot failed in other ways. Despite the attention that some separatist groups have received in recent years through, for example, the film *Witness*, which depicted life amongst the old-order Amish, most immigrant groupings did not formally prohibit integration into the American mainstream. The sects that sought isolation for religious or cultural reasons were relatively small in number. However, it became evident by the 1960s – particularly through the work of Nathan Glazer and Patrick Moynihan – that despite the melting pot, the different ethnic groupings remained 'unmeltable' (Glazer and Moynihan 1967: 290). Indeed, they asserted, some of the differences had become more pronounced over time. This was because many ethnic differences were tied to religious differences:

> The groups do not disappear, however, because of their religious aspect which serves as a basis of a subcommunity, and a subculture. Doctrines and practices are modified to some extent to conform to an American norm, but a distinctive set of values is nurtured in the social groupings defined by religious affiliation. This is quite contrary to early expectations. (Glazer and Moynihan 1967: 313)

There are also difficulties using the concept of the melting pot as a basis for exceptionalism. Other countries have also attracted – and integrated – migrants from different nations. Although the US received 20 per cent of the world's immigrants in 2001, a further 19 per cent were making their way to Europe (Power 2001: 21). Furthermore, as the labour market becomes increasingly globalised, more migrant communities and **diasporas** are being created across the globe.

The frontier

Alongside notions of the melting pot, the work of Frederick Jackson Turner (1863–1932), a history professor at the University of Wisconsin, has also provided a basis for exceptionalist claims. Turner argued – in a paper presented to the American Historical Association in July 1893 – that the frontier marking the settlers' shift westwards across the continent or, as Turner put it, 'the meeting point between savagery and civilization', had imbued American society with its defining characteristics. The frontier – beyond which lay unsettled territory – offered economic opportunity, land to the pioneers who settled there and, by creating a large class of small landowners, extended political power beyond the traditional elites. The frontier also changed attitudes. Turner suggested that the task of taming the environment required the abandonment of European culture and thought. Immigrants from different European countries were compelled to live, work and trade together, establishing a 'composite nationality'. 'In the crucible of the frontier', Turner asserted, '. . . the immigrants were Americanized, liberated, and fused into a mixed race, English in neither nationality or characteristics' (Etulain 1999: 31). Frontier life bred self-reliant individualism. It laid the basis for a restless impatience with accumulated experience, a firm conviction that barriers and

setbacks could always be transcended, and a pronounced hostility to government officialdom:

> That courseness and strength combined with acuteness and inquisitiveness; that
> practical, inventive turn of mind, quick to find expedients; that masterful grasp of
> material things, lacking in the artistic but powerful to effect great ends; that rest-
> less, nervous energy; that dominant individualism, working for good and for evil,
> and withal that buoyancy and exuberance which comes with freedom – these are
> traits of the frontier, or traits called out elsewhere because of the existence of the
> frontier. (Quoted in Etulain 1999: 37)

Some observers have talked of a continuing frontier. Since the end of the nineteenth century it has, they assert, taken a succession of forms including urbanisation, industrialisation, suburbanisation and the adoption of new
technology. Each 'new frontier' has involved a process of pushing outwards
that has – like Turner's original frontier – shaped and structured the overall
character of American society (Elazar 1994: 73–101). The frontier has also
been a recurring theme in popular commentaries. A celebrated description,
scripted seventy years after Turner's address, identified outer space as the 'final
frontier'. The concept has also, nonetheless, been subject to sustained criticism.
The frontier is – according to some observers – a **monocausal** explanation of
American development that draws upon human geography alone. Other processes, such as revolution, war and industrialisation, also played a significant
part in shaping the social and cultural character of the US. In addition, other
societies, including Russia, also had a frontier experience. Much of Siberia had
to be settled. However, the process did not lead to the forging of cultural characteristics such as those ascribed to the US by Turner. Indeed, Russia remained
an authoritarian and hierarchical society.

There are also significant silences regarding gender and race. Turner
appears to be describing the moulding of the white American man. The position of women, African-Americans and native-Americans is largely neglected.
Moreover, few would now accept that the process of 'Americanisation' had the
all-embracing or total character depicted by Turner. Instead, as noted above,
there were large numbers of 'hyphenated' Americans, such as Italian-
Americans or Irish-Americans, who retained a sense of belonging and
primary identification that co-existed alongside notions of an American
identity.

Turner argues that the American West – represented as an untamed and
primal wilderness – brought forth a culture that rested on individualism, resilience and self-reliance. However, the work of recent historians offers a different
picture of frontier life. Mody C. Boatright suggests that, in place of individualism, there was 'a strong corporate feeling' (Boatright 1968: 48). Pioneers were
bound together by folkways, common law and a sense of communality. In
1848, for example, rules emerged among them to regulate the California gold

rush. These rules were informal, but recognised and enforced. Furthermore, as David Wrobel notes, 'revisionist' historians have questioned the extent to which the West was associated with individualism and self-reliance. Instead, they assert, large-scale commercial interests played a predominant role. It was a period of 'capitalist excess' (Wrobel 1993: vii).

A fragment culture

Louis Hartz (1964) offers a different perspective. He argues that European settler societies, such as in the US, Australia, South Africa and Latin America, were constructed around 'fragment cultures'. The colonists were not representative of European society as a whole, but were instead drawn largely from just one grouping, the commercial middle classes. They are described in the language of Marxism as the **bourgeoisie**.

Whereas European societies were still tied down by the remnants of feudalism and the medieval era, fragment societies such as the US broke free. There was neither a landed aristocracy nor a peasantry who were bound to the aristocracy through networks of bonds, obligations and notions of deference. Instead, Hartz suggests, the US represented the purest form of middle-class society in terms of both its social structure and its governing ideology: 'Its individualism is intense, its capitalism aggressive, its "Americanism" doctrinaire. It is . . . the Marxian archetype of the bourgeois fragment' (Hartz 1964: 71). Furthermore, the US remained tied to the defining principles of seventeeth-century liberalism. In essence, time came to a halt: 'the Americans, by the chance conditions of their founding, had slipped free of the underlying motor of historical change. Starting differently, they were fated to be eternally the same – and eternally different from everyone else' (quoted in Rodgers 1988: 29).

The Hartz critique suggests that the contemporary US has been shaped by its formative development. In contrast with Europe, liberal ideologies – which emphasise individualism, self-reliance and laissez-faire – remain dominant. This has important consequences. First, although other reasons played a role (see below), the US lacks a mass socialist movement. Collectivist politics – based upon an extension of government provision – have never taken root. Second, in contrast with Europe, other political traditions have also tended to eschew government interventionism. As Graham K. Wilson records: 'Whereas British Conservatives and continental European Christian Democrats parties speedily accepted the creation of a welfare state that included government-funded health care, American conservatives have never accepted the legitimacy of the welfare state ' (Wilson 1998: 5). Liberal hegemony has therefore had consequences for the overall role of government. When measured as a share of Gross Domestic Product (GDP), US government spends significantly less than in the countries of Europe (see Table 1.1).

Table 1.1   *Government spending, 1970–85 (as a percentage of Gross Domestic Product)*

	1970	1975	1980	1985
US	31.6	34.6	33.7	36.7
Europe	36.6	44.1	45.7	49.2

Source: Adapted from McKenzie and Lee 1991.

Hartz's analysis has been very influential. The claim that the US is a 'pure' liberal society has, however, been subject to criticism. First, other fragment societies – most notably Canada, Australia and the countries of South America – also exist. Some observers suggest that Hartz's analysis fails to explain the distinctive features that characterise each of these societies. Second, the absence of government health care provision and the limited scope of assistance for those in poverty can be attributed to the institutional character of the US political system, not ideological variables. Within a system of checks and balances, power is separated – or, in some accounts, shared – between different institutions. It is therefore simple to block proposed reforms. Third, it is a mistake to generalise about the character of American society. Although liberal thinking had a hold in the northern states, the South had a hierarchical, indeed quasi-feudal character resting on a fixed social order. Fourth, although socialism has never taken root in the US, the differences between popular opinion in the US and that in Europe should not be exaggerated. Some spending programmes, for example, gained a significant degree of popular support, particularly during the period of surplus budgets in the late 1990s. Last, although government spending is proportionately lower in the US than in Europe, it is significantly higher than in Japan.

A people of plenty

In his book, *People of Plenty*, first published in 1954, David M. Potter also sees the US as an exceptional society. However, he regards material abundance as the defining feature of American society. Over the centuries, Potter notes: 'Explorers have marveled at wealth previous undiscovered; travelers have contrasted the riches of America with the scarcity of the lands from which they came; millions of inhabitants of the Old World have responded as immigrants to the lure of the land of plenty, the land of promise' (Potter 1958: 80). This, Potter suggests, has social and political consequences. A free and democratic system is, he asserts, contingent upon the provision of an economic surplus (Potter 1958: 114). Economically underdeveloped societies that condemn most of their citizens to endless toil, drudgery and a bare subsistence living require that their citizens accept the station in life to which they are assigned. Competitive elections – which raise hopes and expectations – cannot therefore be held. In contrast, America's resources and the scale of its economic growth allowed liberty and democracy to flourish. Indeed, Potter asserts, the depth of the American attachment to these principles is such that the nation has seen its national mission in terms of their promulgation across the globe (Potter 1958: 128–41).

American socialism

A number of historians and political scientists have emphasised what they regard as the exceptional character of the American labour movement. First, the American trades union movement has been weak. Even at their peak, the trades unions represented only about a quarter of the workforce (see Table 1.2).

Table 1.2 *Percentage of the labour force in trades unions, 1900–99*

Date	%
1900	3.3
1910	5.9
1920	11.7
1930	7.5
1940	13.1
1950	23
1960	22.3
1970	25.4
1980	19.6
1990	13.3
1999	13.9

Source: Stanley and Niemi 2000:401.

Second, the American unions have generally had an essentially sectional and craft-based character. They have remained confined to particular industries. Furthermore, although they have some ties with the Democratic Party, they have always eschewed class-based politics. Successive studies have drawn contrasts between the US and countries such as France and Germany where trades unionism had – at least during some periods – a more generalised and class-conscious character.

Third, American socialism won relatively few adherents. In Europe, socialist parties emerged during the late nineteenth century. After 1917 it seemed likely that the Bolshevik revolution in Russia would be emulated and there were short-lived soviet republics in Bavaria and Hungary. Socialist parties assumed the reins of government across Europe and communists gained a mass following in a number of countries. The American experience was different. The Socialist Party held its founding convention in 1901. In the 1912 elections, the party's candidate – Eugene V. Debs – gained nearly 6 per cent of the vote. Furthermore, as Irving Howe records, it claimed 118,000 dues-paying members and held over a thousand public offices. Thirteen daily and 262 weekly socialist newspapers were in circulation (Howe 1985: 3). The party gained particular support from four groupings.

- In Wisconsin, German-Americans, many of whom were skilled operatives, were committed to social reform, particularly at a local level.
- In New York, Jewish socialists, led by Morris Hillquit, established themselves among immigrants in districts such as the Lower East Side.
- The Socialist Party also attracted support in southwestern states. In 1912 Eugene Debs gained over 80,000 votes in Oklahoma, Texas, Arkansas and Louisiana. It inherited the populist tradition, and its hostility to those seen as exploiters, but also drew on Christian revivalism.
- In the west, socialists gained the backing of those with more radical ambitions who supported the Industrial Workers of the World. The IWW (or 'Wobblies') was a revolutionary trade union committed to industrial militancy – including mass strikes and sabotage – the overthrow of the employing class and the creation of a socialist society.

However, the 1912 election represented the high-water mark of American socialism rather than a formative stage and, by the end of the decade, the party had collapsed. As Irving Howe records: 'The American socialist movement . . . breathed an aura of hope and expectation . . . Yet, within six or seven years, the Socialist Party would be in shambles, with many of its leaders imprisoned, its organization torn apart by government repression, its ranks split into warring factions, and thousands of the faithful bewildered and demoralized' (Howe 1985: 5–6). Although there was a period of revival during the 1930s, and its presidential candidate, Norman Thomas, gained 2.5 per cent of the vote in 1932, its successes were again short-lived. The party was dissolved in 1963. Although the new left of the late 1960s gave birth to a number of organisations and groupings, they remained at the margins of American politics.

In 1906 a German observer, Werner Sombart, wrote a book that attracted considerable attention. Its title was *Why is there no socialism in the United States?* The question – which can be answered in different ways – is still being asked a century later. Sombart answered his own question by emphasising the availability of free land to those pioneers who – until the closing of the frontier was announced in 1890 – made the journey westwards. It provided, he asserted, a 'safety-valve', releasing some of the social pressures that might otherwise have exacerbated class tensions. Like David M. Potter (1958) fifty years later, Sombart also emphasised the material prosperity of the American working-class. In a celebrated phrase, he wrote that America was 'Canaan, the promised land of capitalism' where 'on the reefs of roast beef and apple pie socialistic utopias of every sort are sent to their doom' (Leon 1971: 238). This had important consequences. In Europe, working-class progress and improved living standards appeared to depend upon the redistribution of wealth from rich to poor and the expropriation of the 'means of production' from the ruling classes. In contrast, in the US social improvement was not regarded as a zero-sum process in which the gains of some had to be matched by the losses of others. This, Potter asserts, was because the country's rate of growth and the opportunities for upward mobility allowed individuals to become prosperous without denuding the wealth of others.

Some argue that the failure of socialism in the US can be rooted in the origins of many of those who migrated to the US from the 1880s onwards. As has been noted, large numbers from southern and eastern Europe made the transatlantic journey. They were rural peasants who had traditionalist and religious attitudes towards life. They were insecure and unsure of their new surroundings. Some looked for security towards the Roman Catholic church which was bitterly opposed to socialist doctrines and labour radicalism. Although, paradoxically, many socialist leaders and organisers were immigrants themselves, the innate conservatism of immigrant life proved resistant to socialist doctrines.

Geographical mobility has always been a distinctive feature of American life. There were, therefore, high levels of turnover and change in working-class neighbourhoods. This prevented the formation of stable institutions and organisations. The American working class was also divided and fragmented. This inhibited the development of class cohesiveness. There were significant ethnic cleavages and regional divisions. The Socialist Party had, for example, to publish its literature in twenty different languages. Furthermore, many working-class migrants from Europe asserted their 'whiteness' – and thus their American identity – through overt hostility to blacks. In California there was also hostility towards Asian-Americans, and many within the labour unions backed the imposition of immigration restrictions.

There were also significant tensions between skilled and unskilled workers. Attempts to bridge the divide invariably failed. Before the 1870s nearly all unions were locally organised and craft-based. Then, in 1881, the Noble and Holy Order of the Knights of Labor opened its ranks to all wage earners. It sought the solidarity of labour and only excluded those regarded as exploiters and speculators. It acted as a trade union movement and a political party seeking a society in which industry was co-operatively owned. It also served as a fraternal organisation pooling resources so as to help members facing illness or other difficulties. By 1886 about 20 per cent of workers were affiliated and strikes erupted in the coal fields and railroad yards. However, the Knights' successes were short-lived. They faced administrative and organisational difficulties, and went into rapid decline.

In many of the European countries, the socialist parties established themselves and won a mass following by being in the forefront of struggles and campaigns to win an extension of the right to vote – or **franchise**. In contrast, in the US, almost all white men had gained the right to vote by the 1830s without a struggle. In a memorable phrase, Selig Perlman described the expansion of the franchise as the 'free gift of the ballot' (Foner 1984: 68).

There are also formidable barriers retarding the development of minor parties – such as socialist organisations – in the US. These include ballot access. In many states, there is a requirement that a minor party should obtain a large number of signatures before being included on the ballot. Congressional elections are organised on a simple plurality – or first-past-the post – basis. This encourages the belief that votes for a minor party will serve little purpose. In addition, The Republicans and Democrats have never had rigid ideological identities. Instead, they have a loose and amorphous character that enables them to absorb new social movements. During the early years of the twentieth century the Democrats expropriated many of the proposals put forward by early socialists, thereby undermining the basis for the formation of an independent party. These included calls for a minimum wage, factory inspection, a system of progressive taxation (by which the proportion of income taken in taxation increases as levels of income rise) and women's suffrage. In the 1930s the New Deal's promise of economic regeneration through public works projects solidified the loyalty of blue-collar workers towards the Democrats.

As noted above, both Louis Hartz and Seymour Martin Lipset have emphasised the extent to which American political culture is characterised by a consensus structured around individualistic values. There is little sense of a common interest binding the working class together. Few would contemplate using the strike weapon to achieve a political goal. Indeed, where disputes arise, they tend to be driven by the aspirations of workers to join the ranks of the middle class. The few dissident socialists and communists who have broken ranks with the consensus have invariably been represented as outcasts and outlaws. Furthermore, when labour protests did assume a political form, they were tied to syndicalism and, in some instances, anarchism. These are essentially individualistic rather than collectivist forms of thinking. The anarchist and syndicalist vision is anti-statist, insofar as it rests upon the dismantling of the governmental apparatus. In contrast, socialism – which won a mass following in European countries such as Germany and France – is structured around an expansion of the government's powers and sphere of responsibility.

Aristide Zolberg emphasises the role of the industrial structure in the failure of socialism in the US. By the beginning of the twentieth century, the US was already becoming a white-collar country. A smaller proportion of the workforce was employed in heavy industry – traditionally a bastion of trade unionism – than in Europe (Zolberg 1988: 109). Moreover, the 'Gompers doctrine' pursued by the trades – or labour – unions enabled workers to make significant gains. Samuel Gompers – originally a New York cigar maker – was president of the American Federation of Labor (AFL) for almost forty years. The AFL was committed to 'pure and simple' trades unionism and short-term economic gains. It eschewed politics and the visions put forward by radicals and socialists and, in contrast with earlier forms of working-class organisation, the AFL survived the difficulties created by recession and the hostility of employers.

The character of the socialist movement itself also deserves attention. It had – perhaps because it was isolated – a sectarian and factional character. The Socialist Party in America, Lipset and Marks (2000) point out, 'was one of the most orthodox Marxist parties in the democratic world'. It stood aside from many of the struggles for higher wages or improved working conditions pursued by the labour unions. Some of its activists similarly derided the 'sewer socialism' of those who pursued municipal reform. The party also opposed the US's entry into the First World War. It was regarded as a conflict between imperialist powers. This stand won backing from some German-Americans and others with ties to the central powers, and the socialist vote rose in the 1917 local elections to 22 per cent, but it isolated socialists from many who supported the war effort (Howe 1985: 41). By the 1930s and 1940s, the Communist Party was the principal organisation on the American left. However, its close associations with the Soviet Union, and its adherence to the twists and turns of Soviet foreign policy, isolated it from workers who might otherwise have been drawn into the party's ranks.

Meanwhile, in Britain, middle-class reformers – who were critical of laissez-faire economics – established the Fabian Society. It joined with others to establish the Labour Party in 1900 and provided many of its leading figures. In contrast, in the US, progressive intellectuals and reformers instead found other political homes.

Together, these factors go some way to answer the question why socialism failed in the US. Nonetheless, although claims that the American labour movement has an exceptionalist character have been widely accepted, they have also been subject to sustained criticism. Some suggest that the contrast drawn between the US and Europe is illusory. First, it underestimates the extent and scale of class-based forms of protest in the US. Second, the degree to which European politics have been informed by social class should also be questioned. As Mary Nolan argues, exceptionalism 'assumes that in the late nineteenth and early twentieth centuries there was a monolithically class-conscious Europe, with strong socialist trade unions and political parties in contrast to an America of business unionism, and two-party, machine politics' (Nolan 1997). This is, as Nolan implies, a misleading picture. Although working-class parties were formed across much of Europe, their radicalism was often tepid. Long before 1914, when almost all the deputies in the Reichstag backed the German war effort, the German Social Democrats' associations with Marxism had become a ritual formality. In Britain, as Ralph Miliband has shown, the Labour Party adopted a moderate platform through much of its history. Even at times of apparent radicalism, its policies could barely be distinguished from the thinking of the Liberal Party that it had displaced. At the same time, the trades unions – or at least their official leaders – always sought to dissociate themselves from the use of the strike weapon for political goals.

Furthermore, there have been instances of widespread industrial militancy and working-class unrest in the US. The IWW – which was committed to the revolutionary overthrow of the employing class – had a mass following. Sean Wilentz argues that although workers often clothed their demands in the language of American tradition rather than international socialism, labour disputes were rooted in class consciousness. They sought to constrain the powers of the employing class. As Wilentz asserts, they were informed by 'a bedrock insistence . . . that American workers had the right to control their labor as something more like a personal estate than like a capitalist commodity' (Wilentz 1984: 18).

There are also claims that socialism did not 'fail' in the US but was instead suppressed. At the time of the First World War and in its aftermath, federal and state government authorities employed 'red scare' tactics. Socialism was defined as 'un-American', militants were jailed, and a number – most notably Joe Hill of the IWW, and the anarchist activists Nicola Sacco and Bartolomeo Vanzetti – were executed after questionable trials. The Left faced a further period of isolation during the McCarthy era of the late 1940s and 1950s. These forms of repression are, it has been argued, obscured by an emphasis upon 'exceptionalism' and the structural characteristics of American society. As DeBrizzi argues: '"American Exceptionalism" as a contemporary ideology is a powerful means toward obscuring the importance of the subjective intervention of the State in the objective social processes of the American political-economic system' (DeBrizzi 1978–79: 93). There was also resolute opposition to radical working-class organisations by employers' associations. Some suggest that the Knights of Labor did not collapse because of sectional tensions but because of the actions (often abetted by government) of employers' associations. In many companies, the trades unions were hounded out through the adoption of an open-shop policy, dubbed the 'America Plan'.

There are other objections to exceptionalist approaches. During the final years of the twentieth century, American political ideas and methods were increasingly adopted in Europe and the distinctions between the continents began to fade. In particular, European socialism appeared to retreat still further from radicalism. After Bill Clinton's electoral success in 1992 and 1996, the Democratic Party in the US began to serve as a model for those in Europe seeking a 'third way' that abandoned the reformist goals and visions of government interventionism that had been adopted in former years. Attempts to represent the absence of a working-class socialist party as a form of exceptionalism became increasingly anachronistic: 'The use of socialism as a test for the presence or absence of exceptionalism has lost its validity as socialism has withered into a fairly mild social democracy all over the West' (Nelles 1997: 754–5).

Finally, as Eric Foner argues, the question 'why is there no socialism in the US' may be inappropriate. It rests on assumptions associated with Marxism, in particular the assertion that class consciousness is a necessary and inevitable consequence of the capitalist order. As Foner observes: 'No one asks, for example, "why is there no feminism in Europe?" . . . because socialism is held to be an inevitable, universal development under capitalism while feminism is assumed to emerge from local contingencies that vary from country to country' (Foner 1984: 74).

The exceptional character of US politics

Other exceptionalist accounts of American history and development emphasise the distinctive character of the policy-making process. Although elements drawn from the American system have been reproduced by other countries across the world, Byron E. Shafer refers to the exceptionalism of US governmental structures. First, separation of powers – through which power is divided between the executive, legislative and judicial branches of government – is more pronounced and takes a more institutionalised form in the US than in other countries. Second, the federal courts play a pivotal role in interpreting the Constitution. As Shafer records: 'Many of the great issues in post-war politics – civil rights, civil liberties, electoral apportionment, criminal justice, religion in public life, the regulation of private morality, even the balance between the executive and legislature – have been principally the province of the Court' (Shafer 1989: 590). Third, there is the primary election. This takes place at the pre-nomination stage of the electoral process and allows the public to participate in the process of candidate selection by the parties. It weakens the party apparatus and encourages a form of political entrepreneurship in which individuals organise their own campaigns and seek out local preferences.

The American 'creed'

There are other ways of understanding exceptionalism and the distinctiveness of American society. The US has been described as **ideational**. In contrast with the nations of Europe and Asia, national identity rests upon shared ideas, beliefs and principles rather than the 'blood ties' of family connections or a culture derived from networks of closely bound folkways. Some observers have, on this basis, drawn a comparison between the US and the former Soviet Union. Soviet identity was based upon a commitment to the principles of Marxism-Leninism. Although its defining principles differ profoundly from those of the Soviet Union, the *raison d'être* of the US is also ideological. As Richard Hofstadter remarked in a celebrated phrase, 'It has been our fate as a nation not to have ideologies, but to be one' (quoted in Lipset 1993: 122). What is the character of the American ideology, or as the Swedish sociologist Gunnar Myrdal termed it, 'creed'? Seymour Martin Lipset suggests that it has five component parts (Lipset 1997: 19).

Liberty

The US emerged through a process of revolution. British colonial rule was overthrown by an armed people and, against this background, the established patterns of respect, loyalty and deference towards elite rule were destroyed. Instead, there was a disdain for authority and an emphasis upon the freedom of the individual. This is evident, for example, in the entrenchment of individual rights. The first ten amendments to the Constitution – which became the Bill of Rights – included freedom of speech, freedom of religion, an assurance that those accused of a criminal offence would be accorded 'due' process' of law, and the right to 'bear arms'. This shaped the subsequent history of the US. American culture has been pervaded by an emphasis on the rights of the individual. However, in contrast with the positive rights bestowed in Western Europe particularly after the Second World War (such as the right to an education or health provision) these rights have almost always had a negative character. They offer freedom from the powers of government.

Egalitarianism

Some early visitors to the US, most notably Tocqueville, asserted that egalitarianism was the country's principal defining feature. In his commentaries he referred to 'the general equality of condition among the people'. For Tocqueville, this was 'the fundamental fact from which all others seem to be derived' (quoted in Huntington 1982: 5). However, this is misleading. Although there may have been less inequality among white males during the first half of the nineteenth century than in Europe, there have always been widespread disparities in terms of both income and wealth.

However, American culture has been marked – within defined parameters – by an equality of regard. From the days preceding the revolution, European and Asian notions of deference and social rank found little place. The US Constitution prohibited the granting of hereditary titles. Instead of assuming the patterns of speech and mannerisms associated with social class differences, people spoke to each other as equals. Some Europeans were aghast. Charles Dickens complained that 'everybody talks to you' (quoted in Wiebe 1995: 46). When the English woman Mrs Frances Trollope visited the US in 1830 she was struck by the 'coarse familiarity, untempered by a shadow of respect, which is assumed by the grossest and lowest in their intercourse with the highest and most refined' (quoted in Ashbee and Ashford 1999: 23). Similarly, at the beginning of the twentieth century, Werner Sombart noted: 'America is a freer and more egalitarian society than Europe . . . there is not the stigma of being the class apart that almost all European workers have about them . . . The bowing and scraping before the "upper classes", which produces such an unpleasant impression in Europe, is completely unknown' (quoted in Lipset and Marks 2000: 26).

Alexis de Tocqueville (1805–59)

Tocqueville was born into a French aristocratic family. Despite this, and his fear of revolution, he saw the future of politics in terms of growing equality and democracy. His interest in politics led him to visit the US. On his first journey he stayed nine months, visiting cities such as New York and Boston, and the frontier areas of Michigan and Wisconsin. He talked to President Andrew Jackson, former president John Quincy Adams, the lawyer and politician Daniel Webster and many others. His observations – which drew contrasts between an aristocratic and a democratic system of government – were published in two volumes. The first of these had an optimistic tone, overestimating the extent to which there was equality in the ante-bellum (pre-Civil War) US. The second volume was more pessimistic and conveyed the fear that excessive individualism might undermine citizenship. Tocqueville's work is regarded, however, as pivotal to an understanding of the early American republic and its subsequent evolution.

During the Second World War (1939–45) large numbers of American servicemen were stationed in Britain. Studies record that few felt 'at home socially'. This was because they did not defer and were, by British standards, over-assertive towards those in authority (McElroy 1999: 69). These patterns have continued. Although British society has become markedly less deferential since the 1960s, and is increasingly characterised by a greater informality, a more recent press report highlighted the cultural differences between the two nations. On her visit to the US in 1991, Queen Elizabeth II was introduced to a householder who welcomed her with the phrase 'how are you doin?' (McElroy 1999: 70).

Individualism

Individualism stresses the primacy of the individual. In policy terms, it implies that people should be self-reliant and dependent upon their own efforts rather than on collective provision through the government. Individualism is also tied to **anti-statism**, a suspicion of both government and large-scale forms of organisation. Furthermore, those committed to individualist approaches reject representations of society or history in terms of social classes or group interests (see Chapter 2). Some observers have, however, questioned the extent to which individualism has roots in American history. They argue that there was a long tradition of local communalism and that the **founding fathers** – who wrote the US Constitution in 1787 – were guided by republican notions of civic purpose and duty rather than thoughts of individual self-interest. Individuals, it was thought, owed an obligation to the common good (Kingdon 1999: 27–8).

Populism

Populism – which Lipset identifies as the fourth component of the American creed – emphasises the role of the ordinary citizen, sometimes dubbed the 'little guy'. In its most radical form, populism asserts that workers, farmers and small business owners create the nation's wealth and that their labour is exploited by bankers, landlords and speculators. Often, there is a fear of conspiracies between wealthy elites, foreign interests and those holding positions of political power.

In what ways has populism shaped American politics and popular culture? Lipset argues that although the political process is always constrained by the rule of law, there are opportunities for direct participation by the people. Those serving in the US House of Representatives face the electorate every two years. Whereas European political systems generally have elections for only a limited number of posts, with a process of appointment for other positions, many American state constitutions allow for election to a wide range of different public offices. In some instances, judges are directly elected. Many relatively minor positions, such as membership of school boards, are also subject to election. In many states, referenda are used to determine state policy or to countermand a decision reached in the state legislature. In some states, those who are elected can be subject to a recall procedure. If a petition attracts a sufficient number of signatures from voters, legislators must face a further election if they are to continue in office. Similarly, term limits are imposed in many states to prevent those who are elected serving for unlimited periods and becoming detached from those they represent.

These populist strains are also evident in American popular culture. Countless songs, books and films rest on the tensions between ordinary, honest and dedicated individuals or communities and the uncaring greed of exploitative elites. Much of Bruce Springsteen's music is tied to the plight of blue-collar America. Frank Capra's 1946 film *It's a Wonderful Life* pitted a despairing citizen against a ruthless property owner, and showed that without the vigilance of George Bailey, a selfless citizen played by James Stewart, the town would have become the personal property of the avaricious Mr Potter. More recent films, most notably Oliver Stone's *JFK* and *Nixon*, are structured around assertions that public policy is shaped by a hidden sub-government organised around senior military figures and those controlling the large corporations. Stephen Soderbergh's film *Erin Brockovich* (2000) told of a woman's struggle against a soulless corporation.

Laissez-faire

Laissez-faire is the belief that government should play only a minimal role in economic affairs. Business and commercial decision making should, it is said, be left to the free market. There should, therefore, be little regulation of industry and taxation should be kept at low levels. Although the New Deal and Great Society programmes, of the 1930s and 1960s respectively, extended the economic role of government, they were tied to notions of individual progress rather than collective well-being. As Hugh Heclo records, they were: 'wrapped up in a concept of opportunity for the disadvantaged that seemed full in tune with the American political philosophy' (quoted in Kingdon 1999: 46).

The case for laissez-faire is usually presented in both moral and **consequentialist** terms. Government, it is said, has no right to interfere with privately held property or agreements between individuals drawn up on the basis of mutual consent. Decisions to buy or sell goods, services and labour are essentially private matters. Furthermore, laissez-faire advocates assert, government interventionism has damaging economic consequences. It leads to market distortions, creating either excess supply or excess demand. In contrast, big government requires high levels of taxation that stifle private initiative and place upward pressures on interest rates.

Laissez-faire is widely endorsed in the US. Lipset cites a 1985–6 study showing that there is markedly less public support for government interventionism in the US than in other advanced industrial nations. Whereas 67 per cent of Italians backed statutory price controls, they were endorsed by only 19 per cent in the US. While 85 per cent of British respondents backed government provision of health care, it only won 40 per cent support among Americans (Lipset 1997: 75).

The US and Canada

Lipset and his co-thinkers suggest that liberty and the other components of the creed were born in the American revolution. They argue that there are, therefore, striking differences between the US and Canada. In contrast with the US, Canada was the country of counter-revolution. It remained loyal to the British Crown, maintaining its respect for authority and established hierarchies. In Lipset's words, 'Americans are descended from winners, Canadians . . . from losers' (Lipset 1991:1). All of this shaped the subsequent history and character of the two societies. Alexis de Tocqueville visited Canada in 1831. As H. V. Nelles records, he found it 'quite unexceptional, altogether too much like Europe, beset by a suspicious, joyfully unambitious peasantry, envious of the neighbours. Canadians were definitely not New Men in the eyes of French visitors' (Nelles 1997: 756).

In particular, Canada is less individualistic and more deferential towards government. Lipset illustrates the contemporary differences in culture between the US and Canada by recounting the fate of metrification programmes. At the beginning of the 1970s both nations announced that they would adopt metric in place of imperial systems of measurement:

Canadians were told to go metric and they did. Americans were told to go metric
and they didn't . . . Canadians respect the state, are obedient. They're the country
in a counter-revolution, the country which preserved the monarchy. The United
States is the country which overthrew the state and which is anti-statist and dis-
obedient, and much more lawless. (PBS Online Backgrounders 1996)

Furthermore, although the creed has not remained in an unchanged form over
the past two centuries, its essential tenets still remain in place.

The Great Depression introduced a 'social democratic tinge' in America to quote
Richard Hofstadter. Massive immigration brought large numbers of Catholics and
Lutherans with a hierarchical state church background, as well as millions of
Jews. The Catholics and Jews are communitarian and have helped undermine the
individualistic self-help sectarian tradition. But the original cultural emphases on
antistatism, individualism, egalitarianism, and populism have remained. (Lipset
2000)

However, many of those who describe US national identity in terms of the
creed concede that there has always been a gulf between the ideals associated
with the creed and the institutions constructed on the basis of it. As Samuel P.
Huntington has recorded (1982), the creed was not extended to African-
Americans for almost two centuries. Indeed, for much of this time, they were
denied the most basic rights of citizenship. Although there have been four
periods of 'creedal passion' – such as the civil rights era of the 1950s and 1960s
– when reformers sought to close the gap, there is still a gulf between ideology
and practice.

Seymour Martin Lipset's ideas have been very influential. Nonetheless, the
representations of the US on which his studies rest have been subject to sustained criticism. For some, the distinctions that are drawn between Americans,
Canadians, European and Japanese citizens depend upon ethnic and national
caricatures. They have only a shallow basis in reality. As H. V. Nelles remarks:
'Lipset's work gives a pseudo-scientific basis to some of the clichés and common-
places of our respective national stereotypes' (Nelles 1997: 755). Lipset has also
been accused of offering description as a substitute for explanation. His emphasis upon the process of revolution is not, it is said, sufficient to explain the
contrasting cultural characters of the US and Canada (Conway 1991: 311).

Lipset's descriptions of Canada have, in particular, been subject to challenge.
He implies that particular national values – derived from 'counter-revolution'
– are shared across the country. However, Canada is characterised by ethnic
and cultural diversity. A majority of those in Quebec are French speaking and
there has been widespread support for secession. Yet, as one reviewer remarks,
'Lipset's Canada seems to be a Canada without Quebec' (Nelles 1997: 754).

In identifying values such as individualism as the core of American identity,
observers such as Huntington and Lipset are said by critics to be generalising

from the experience of the early white Protestants. However, they were simply one grouping. Other migrants – particularly those drawn from other religious traditions – held profoundly different ideas and folkways. Many did not share the sense of individualism that is closely associated with the Protestant faith. Instead, they placed greater emphasis on notions of community and collective responsibility.

Claims that the US is an 'ideational state', structured around principles rather than a shared culture or a line of descent, are also open to question. A 1996 survey of public opinion conducted in twenty-four countries by the International Social Survey Program suggested that, for most Americans, national identity depended upon more than ideology. To be 'truly American', two-thirds of those questioned asserted, individuals must have been born in the US. Over 70 per cent said that they should have lived in the US for most of their life. There was overwhelming agreement with the proposition that to be 'truly American' a person must speak English. Furthermore, over half asserted that Americanism rested on acceptance of the Christian faith (Ashbee 2002).

The exceptionalism of America's national purpose

Other observers have emphasised America's sense of a national mission. The civil rights protests were, for example, informed by a sense that the collective purpose of the nation had to be fulfilled. As Sacvan Bercovitch notes: 'The problem was not what's usually called identity. These people never asked "Who are we?", but, as though deliberately avoiding that commonsense question, "when is our errand to be fulfilled?"' (Bercovitch 1981: 6).

The 'errand', according to Bercovitch, is derived from the theological thinking of some amongst the earliest Puritan settlers. Although those who landed at the Plymouth Rock in 1620 – who are celebrated as the founders of America – were 'separating' Congregationalists who had turned their backs on the sins and corruption of the Old World, others – most notably those who sailed with John Winthrop ten years afterwards and established a settlement at Boston – were 'non-separating' Congregationalists. Citing the work of historians such as Perry Miller, Deborah L. Madsen records:

> The Puritan colonists did not so much flee persecution in England as they went to Massachusetts in order to work out the complete transformation of the church begun but not completed in England and Europe, for the reason that the reformers had no model as their guide. It was this model that the Puritan colonists intended to provide. So New England would be exemplary, God would bless the new land and the newly perfected church, and the temporary colonials would return to govern the perfectly reformed church in England. According to John Winthrop, the colonists were charged with the responsibility of proving the ways of God to man, no less. (Madsen 1998: 10)

The 'errand' imposed a strict discipline upon the colonists. There was always a sense of God's watching presence and an awareness of the constant need for collective self-discipline. Calamities such as disease, famine and war were regarded as a sign from God that the colonists had failed to lead their lives in a proper way. Successive 'jeremiads' warned that wordliness could corrupt colonists and jeopardise the success of the 'errand'. The persecution of alleged witches ensured that the communities remained tightly bound, despite the fragmenting effects of frontier life and trading relationships (Madsen 1998: 12).

In a phrase that has often been recalled, and was cited by President Reagan, Winthrop proclaimed that the settlement he had built would serve as a beacon to the people of Europe: 'Wee shall be as a Citty upon a Hill, the eies of all people are uppon us' (quoted in Davis and Lynn-Jones 1987: 22). In the eighteenth century, as the Puritans became 'Yankees', such notions began to be understood in secular rather than in purely theological terms. The belief that Americans had a part to play in the regeneration of humanity was however interpreted in different ways. Some believed that the 'City upon a Hill' depended for its survival on a degree of isolation. The US would therefore stand aside from the foreign entanglements. As John Quincy Adams – who was to serve as the sixth president – said in an 1821 speech, the country's hearts and prayers would always be with those seeking freedom and independence, the US would not impose its principles upon others: 'But she goes not abroad in search of monsters to destroy . . . She will recommend the general cause by the countenance of her voice, and by the benignant sympathy of her example' (quoted in Baritz 1985: 13). Thinking such as this contributed to an **isolationist** foreign policy. This was adopted by successive administrations for much of American history, most notably during the inter-war years.

Some suggest, however, that the sense of national purpose bequeathed by the early settlers contributed to periods of expansionism as well as isolationism. Many argue that the US had a responsibility not only to lead by example, but to bring principles such as freedom and democracy to an oppressive, corrupt and unenlightened world. As Loren Baritz puts it: 'In countless ways Americans know in their gut . . . that we have been Chosen to lead the world in public morality and to instruct it in political virtue. We believe that our own domestic goodness results in strength adequate to destroy our opponents who, by definition, are enemies of virtue, freedom, and God' (Baritz 1985: 11). During the nineteenth century this provided an ideological basis for territorial expansion across the American continent and the absorption of the territories that were occupied into the US – a process hailed in 1845 by John L. O'Sullivan, editor of *Democratic Review*, as the country's 'manifest destiny'.

By the beginning of the twentieth century these sentiments led to calls for the 'export' of democracy, freedom and national independence. It has been argued that the US's conception of itself as a 'redeemer nation' lay behind President Woodrow Wilson's attempts – as the First World War came towards its close – to reconstruct Europe. He rejected the empire-building and amoral power politics of the major powers and instead committed himself to the rights of small nations (often termed 'national self-determination'). He wanted to rebuild Europe on American lines. As Gordon Levin notes:

> With the evils of militarism and pre-liberal reaction left behind in Europe, America had an historic mission to disseminate the progressive values of liberal-internationalism and to create a new world order. In Wilson's completely liberal ideology, imperialism and militarism were seen as essentially European phenomena associated with a past which America had escaped . . . America was for Wilson the incarnation of the progressive future of European politics and diplomacy, after Europe had cast off the burdens of its militant and pre-bourgeois past in favor of more rational, liberal-capitalist development. (Gordon Levin, quoted in Perlmutter 1997: 30–1)

Those who define exceptionalism in terms of America's world role argue that in the latter half of the twentieth century messianic visions of national purpose contributed to the American assumption of global leadership. As Cold War tensions between the West and the Soviet Union grew, the US guaranteed the security of non-communist nations. Some commentators went further and suggested that communism – which had been imposed across Eastern Europe and much of Asia in the late 1940s – could be 'rolled back'. The US would, as President John F. Kennedy assured the world in his 1961 inaugural speech, 'pay any price, bear any burden, meet any hardship, support any friend, oppose any foe to assure the survival and the success of liberty'. In the 1960s these beliefs led the US towards military intervention in South-East Asia. Michael Hunt is one of a number of observers to attribute US involvement to the sense of purpose that the country had inherited from its founders. He records that 'by 1967, half a million Americans, moved by dreams and fears as old as their nation and yet still as fresh as yesterday, were fighting in Vietnam' (Hunt 1987: 170).

Although the end of the Cold War – and the collapse of the Soviet bloc – led to uncertainty about the American role in the world, some policy makers believed that the US had continuing international responsibilities. It should, they argued, promote democratic values and procedures, particularly among the countries of Eastern Europe. According to Henry Kissinger, who served as National Security Adviser and Secretary of State in the Nixon and Ford administrations, 'Wilsonianism seemed triumphant' (quoted in J. Dumbrell unpublished paper).

Some observers have, however, sought to qualify the importance of notions of America as a 'redeemer nation'. They have questioned the claim that US foreign policy has been governed by 'exceptionalist' principles. For example, the role of the Puritan settlers in shaping the subsequent history of American can be over-emphasised. Although Puritanism shaped the history of New England, the South and West were governed by different ideological traditions. Other critics suggest that although the US may have regarded itself as a 'promised land', its foreign policy commitments were driven by traditional notions of *real-politik* – practical politics – rather than by a messianic commitment to the liberation of foreign lands. Walter A. McDougall asserts, for example, that the actions of the US were essentially pragmatic responses to opportunities and the ambitions of others. In particular, he emphasises, the expansion of the US across the continent was not driven by idealism or a sense of 'manifest destiny' but was, instead, the inevitable consequence of a growing population and commercial opportunity. As McDougall puts it: 'US expansion needs no explanation. Geography invited it; demography compelled it' (McDougall 1997: 79). It was only at the end of the nineteenth century, McDougall suggests, that notions of the US as a 'crusader state' began to hold sway. At this time, Progressive impulses led to an 'imperialism of righteousness' and efforts to promote American ideals across the globe.

Arthur M. Schlesinger Jr acknowledges the role played by notions of America as a chosen or 'redeemer' nation, but argues that they were held in check by uncertainty and insecurity. Many of the founding fathers – who wrote the US Constitution in 1787 – were influenced by the classical era and the fate of ancient Rome. Their minds were occupied by thoughts of a republic – ruled by law but also shaped by the active participation of at least some citizens – that had collapsed, leading to autocracy, imperial ambition, hubris and eventual disintegration. The creation of the US therefore represented an attempt to defy historical precedent. In the words of the US historian Henry Adams: 'The men who made the Constitution . . . intended to make by its means an issue with antiquity' (quoted in Schlesinger 1999: 10–11). Schlesinger argues that as the nineteenth century progressed and the republic became more certain of itself, the notion of America as an experiment – and the sense of vulnerability that it induced – lost much of its former influence. Instead, the idea – bequeathed by the Puritans – of the US as a chosen country with what he terms 'the delusion of a sacred mission and a sanctified destiny' held sway (Schlesinger 1999: 16). However, at times, the fears of the founding fathers re-emerged in either dark forecasts of American decline or profound uncertainty about the future. President John F. Kennedy issued a warning in his first annual message: 'Before my term has ended . . . we shall have to test anew whether a nation organized and governed such as ours can endure. The outcome is by no means certain' (quoted in Schlesinger 1999: 20).

Although successive presidents talked of America's role in the Cold War as an exceptionalist crusade for freedom, some on both the right and the left reject this. They suggest instead that the US was – like other powers – guided by perceptions of its own economic and strategic self-interest. Its actions during the Cold War were not inspired by the redemption of the world, but by commercial and national security considerations. After 1945 the US simply redefined its own sphere of vital interest so that it extended to the Elbe, which had become the dividing line between Western and Eastern Europe. Similarly, although policy makers talked of democracy promotion during the 1990s, this cloaked commercial and military considerations.

Exorcising exceptionalism

Each of the eight forms of exceptionalism has been the subject of sustained criticism. However, there are those who question the fundamental legitimacy of the concept. They put forward four further arguments.

First, 'exceptionalism' suggests, by definition, that a country has a unique national character. National character is, however, a problematic concept. There are methodological and logistical difficulties: 'It implies . . . some singular ethos or mystique. Catching hold of such an ethos firmly by the tail is difficult enough with smaller societies such as Samoa, Sumatra, or Liechtenstein; with a large and heterogeneous people, it is well nigh impossible' (Kammen 1993: 3).

Others assert that studies structured around the nation always underestimate or disregard cleavages within nations, such as those derived from class, gender, ethnicity and race. Indeed, radical observers would suggest that disadvantaged groupings in different countries share more with each other than they have in common with others in their own country. They talk, for example, of an international working class. Furthermore, recent critiques have suggested that although notions of a national identity may have had a degree of validity in the past, this has now been lost. In the contemporary era, it is said, individuals have multiple identities tied to particular lifestyles and cultural formations. These exist 'below' and, as the globalisation process has advanced, 'above' the nation state. Stuart Hall notes the ways in which they mesh together and overlap: 'Identities are fragmented and fractured, never singular but multiply constructed across different, often intersecting and antagonistic, discourses, practices and positions' (quoted in Isin and Wood 1999: 16).

Third, the claim that the US has distinct characteristics that mark it out from all other nations can be applied to many other nations. For example, a number of observers – particularly those influenced by Marxist thinking – have emphasised the 'exceptional' character of German economic and social development. They speak of a *Sonderweg* or special path. Whereas the growth of industrial capitalism is traditionally associated with the emergence of liberal-democratic institutions, German industrialisation took place within an authoritarian regime dominated by feudal landlords. There have similarly been claims that Britain is 'exceptional'. Its 'bourgeois revolution' was also stunted. In many other countries, an increasingly influential class of merchants and industrialists (the 'bourgeoisie') overthrew the feudal landlords and the monarchy. The French revolution is regarded as prototypical. In Britain, however, the bourgeoisie made its peace with the *ancien régime* at an early stage and some vestiges of feudalism – such as the monarchy, the House of Lords, and notions of deference – remained in place.

Finally, the concept of exceptionalism also rests – as noted above – on the notion that there is a common standard, shared path or 'law' against which the historical development of nations can be judged. As Joyce Appleby puts it: 'There are no exceptions without well-understood generalizations or norms in contrast to which the exception commands attention' (quoted in Appleby 1992: 23). However, the idea of historical laws or norms is increasingly regarded as anachronistic. Marxism – which in at least its classical form – rested on laws of history that culminated in working-class revolution and the creation of a socialist order, has been largely discredited by the collapse of states claiming adherence to communist principles and the apparent resilience of world capitalism. While alternative theories of historical development have been advanced, they have only received a lukewarm reception. Francis Fukuyama, author of *The End of History*, argues that industrialisation and modernisation lead inexorably to the growth of civil society, free market economies and liberal democracy. There is, Fukuyama claims, a process leading to 'a certain uniformity of economic and political institutions across different regions and cultures' (Fukuyama 1997: 146). However, his arguments have been greeted with considerable scepticism and many observers instead emphasise the differences between nations and the essential irrationality of the historical process. Their claims have been strengthened by the growth of militant Islam.

Loss of faith

Criticisms of American exceptionalism such as these have undermined the idea that the US is in some way 'special'. Alongside the process of disillusionment, there has been a progressive loss of faith in the ideas and institutions that once defined American identity. From the 1960s onwards, many established moral certainties and cultural forms seemed to be crumbling away. Certainly, the promise of economic opportunity and upward mobility – traditionally dubbed the American dream' – lost much of its former credibility. Increasingly, the US appeared to be a class society where individuals were confined to the circumstances into which they had been born. The individualism and commitment to open expression that had once marked out the national character seemed to have been lost. Some asserted that America had become a more conformist society.

There were also suggestions that local communities – another bedrock of traditional American identity – were fragmenting and that there was a process of civic decline. In particular, voluntary associations and organisations seemed to be losing members and individuals appeared increasingly isolated from each other. For some, this has led to a **hyperindividualist** culture in which all seek gains for themselves regardless of others. The family was also said to be in decline. Many observers, most notably those associated with the conservative right, asserted that the country faced a profound moral crisis. They pointed, in particular, to rising divorce and illegitimacy rates and the decline of the 'intact' family.

At the same time, there were claims that the assertions of ethnic and racial identity that followed the civil rights revolution and the dramatic growth in immigrant numbers were leading to the break-up – or **Balkanisation** – of the US. Many observers also argued that the states, localities, and regions had lost their former significance. Conservatives, in particular, asserted that the national government – or 'federal leviathan' – had disregarded 'states' rights' and eradicated established forms of identity.

Subsequent chapters assess these 'jeremiads', survey the evolution of American society during the 1990s, and consider the cultural, economic and social consequences of the terrorist attacks on September 11th 2001.

Summary

The US is often seen in exceptionalist terms. The country has, it is said, followed a separate and distinct path of development. There are, however, different ways of understanding American exceptionalism. Some have cited the character of the American people and the role of the 'melting pot'. Others stress the role of the westward frontier in shaping the American character, the class origins of the American colonies and the absence of a mass socialist party. The basis of American national identity has also attracted a considerable number of studies. In contrast with other countries, some argue, American identity rests upon adherence to particular beliefs and principles rather than family origins. Other observers point to the exceptionalist character of American foreign policy. The Puritan origins of the New England colonies, it has been suggested, imbued the US with a global mission and sense of moral purpose. The concept of American exceptionalism has, however, been subject to intense scrutiny and criticism.

References and further reading

Adams, W. P. (1980), 'The melting pot, assimilation, Americanisation, and other concepts: American public debate concerning the immigration problem, 1890–1930', in R. Kroes (ed.), *The American Identity: Fusion and Fragmentation*, Amsterdam, Amerika Institut – Universiteit van Amsterdam, 215–34.

Appleby, J. (1992) 'Recovering America's historic diversity: beyond exceptionalism', *The Journal of American History*, September, 419–31.

Ashbee, E. (2002), *'Being American': Representations of National Identity*, unpublished paper delivered to the Political Studies Association – American Politics Group, 28th Annual Conference, University of Essex, January 2002.

Ashbee, E. and N. Ashford (1999), *US Politics Today*, Manchester, Manchester University Press.

Baritz, L. (1985), *Backfire: A History of How American Culture Led Us into Vietnam and Made Us Fight the Way We Did*, New York, Ballantine Books.

Bellah, R. N., R. Madsen, W. M. Sullivan, A. Swidler and S. M. Tipton (1985), *Habits of the Heart: Individualism and Commitment in American Life*, Berkeley, University of California Press.

Bender, T. (1993), *Community and Social Change in America*, Baltimore, John Hopkins University Press.

Bercovitch, S. (1981), 'The rites of assent: rhetoric, ritual, and the ideology of the American consensus', in S. B. Girgus (ed.), *The American Self: Myth, Ideology, and Popular Culture*, Albuquerque, University of New Mexico Press, 5–42.

Boatright, M. C. (1968), 'The myth of frontier individualism', in R. Hofstadter and S. M. Lipset (eds), *Turner and the Sociology of the Frontier*, New York, BasicBooks, 43–64.

Conway, J. F. (1991), 'Canada and the US: what makes us different? A response to Seymour Martin Lipset', *Labour / Le Travail*, 28, Autumn, 311–21.

Davis T. R. and S. M. Lynn-Jones (1987), 'Citty upon a hill', *Foreign Policy*, 66, 20–38.

DeBrizzi, J. (1978–9), 'The concept of American exceptionalism as ideology', *Berkeley Journal of Sociology*, 23, 83–98.

Degler, C. N. (1962), *Out of our Past: The Forces that Shaped Modern America*, New York, Harper and Row.

Elazar, D. J. (1994), *The American Mosaic: The Impact of Space, Time, and Culture on American Politics*, Boulder, Westview Press.

Etulain, R. W. (ed.) (1999), *Does the Frontier Experience Make America Exceptional?* (Historians at Work), New York, Bedford Books/St Martin's Press.

Foner, E. (1984), 'Why is there no socialism in the United States?', *History Workshop*, 17, Spring, 57–80.

Frederickson, G. M. (1995), 'From exceptionalism to variability: recent developments in cross-national comparative history', *The Journal of American History*, September, 587–604.

Fukuyama, F. (1997), 'The illusion of exceptionalism', *Journal of Democracy*, 8:3, 146–9.

General Social Survey (1996), *ISSP Module – National Identity*, www.icpsr.umich.edu/GSS

Glazer, N. and D. P. Moynihan (1967), *Beyond the Melting Pot: The Negroes, Puerto Ricans, Jews, Italians and Irish of New York City*, Cambridge, MA, The MIT Press.

Gleason, P. (1980), 'American identity and Americanization', in S. Thernstrom (ed.), *Harvard Encyclopedia of American Ethnic Groups*, Cambridge, MA, Harvard University Press, 31–58.

Greene J. P. (1993), *The Intellectual Construction of America*, Chapel Hill, University of North Carolina Press.

Hartz, L. (1964), *The Founding of New Societies*, San Diego, Harcourt Brace Jovanovich.

Hess, A. (2000), *American Social and Political Thought*, Edinburgh, Edinburgh University Press.

Higham, J. (1999), 'Cultural responses to immigration', in N. J. Smelser and J. C. Alexander (eds), *Diversity and its Discontents: Cultural Conflict and Common Ground in Contemporary American Society*, Princeton, Princeton University Press, 39–61.

Howe, I. (1985), *Socialism and America*, San Diego, Harcourt Brace Jovanovich.

Hunt, M. H. (1987), *Ideology and US Foreign Policy*, New Haven, Yale University Press.

Huntington, S. P. (1982), 'American ideals versus American institutions', *Political Science Quarterly*, Spring, 1–37.

Isin, E. F. and P. K. Wood (1999), *Citizenship and Identity*, London, Sage Publications.

Kammen, M. (1993), 'The problem of American exceptionalism: a reconsideration', *American Quarterly*, 45:1, March, 1–43.

Kingdon, J. W. (1999), *America the Unusual*, New York, St Martin's/Worth.

Leon, D. H. (1971), 'Review: Whatever happened to an American socialist party? A critical survey of the spectrum of interpretations', *American Quarterly*, 23:2, May, 236–58.

Lepgold J. and T. McKeown (1995), 'Is American foreign policy exceptional? An empirical analysis', *Political Science Quarterly*, Autumn, 369–84.

Lipset, S. M. (1991), *Continental Divide: The Values and Institutions of the United States and Canada*, New York, Routledge.

Lipset, S. M. (1993), 'Pacific divide: American exceptionalism – Japanese uniqueness', *International Journal of Public Opinion Research*, 5:2, Summer, 121–66.

Lipset, S. M. (1995), 'Trade union exceptionalism: the United States and Canada', *The Annals of the American Academy of Political and Social Science*, 538, March, 115–130.

Lipset, S. M. (1997), *American Exceptionalism: A Double-Edged Sword*, New York, W. W. Norton.

Lipset, S. M. and G. Marks (2000), *It Didn't Happen Here: Why Socialism Failed in the United States*, New York, W. W. Norton.

Madsen, D. L. (1998), *American Exceptionalism*, Edinburgh, Edinburgh University Press (BAAS Paperbacks).

McDougall, W. A. (1997), *Promised Land, Crusader State*, Boston, Houghton Mifflin.

McElroy, J. H. (1999), *American Beliefs: What Keeps a Big Country and a Diverse People United*, Chicago, Ivan R. Dee.

McKenzie, R. B. and D. R. Lee (1991), *Government in Retreat*, National Center for Policy Analysis, Policy Report no. 97, www.ncpa.org/studies/s164/s164.html

Miliband, R. (1973), *Parliamentary Socialism: A Study in the Politics of Labour*, London, Merlin Press.

Morone, J. A. (1997), 'American exceptionalism: a double-edged sword', *Political Science Quarterly*, Autumn, 506–7.

Nelles, H. V. (1997), 'Review essay: American exceptionalism: a double-edged sword', *American Historical Review*, June, 749–57.

Nolan, M. (1997), 'Against exceptionalisms', *American Historical Review*, June, 769–74.

PBS Online Backgrounders (1996), *American Exceptionalism*, 11 March, www.pbs.org/newshour/gergen/lipset.html

Perlmutter, A. (1997), *Making the World Safe for Democracy: A Century of Wilsonianism and its Totalitarian Challengers*, Chapel Hill, University of North Carolina Press.

Potter, D. M. (1958), *People of Plenty: Economic Abundance and the American Character*, Chicago, University of Chicago Press.

Power, C. (2001), 'Out of the shadows' *Newsweek*, 13 August, 28–30.

Ramalho de Sousa Santos, M. I. (1994), 'American exceptionalism and the naturalization of "America"', *Prospects: An Annual of American Cultural Studies*, 19, 1–23.

Rodgers, D. T. (1988), 'Exceptionalism', in Anthony Molho and Gordon S. Wood (eds), *Imagined Histories: American Historians Interpret Their Past*, Princeton, Princeton University Press, 21–40.

Schlesinger, A. M. Jr, (1999), *The Cycles of American History*, Boston, Houghton Mifflin.

Schwarz, B. (1998), 'Exporting the myth of a liberal America', *World Policy Journal*, 15:3, Autumn, 69–77.

Shafer B. E. (1989), "Exceptionalism" in American politics?', *PS: Political Science and Politics*, 22:3, September, 588–94.

Sowell, T. (1981), *Ethnic America: A History*, New York, BasicBooks.

Stanley, H. W. and Niemi, R. G. (2000) *Vital Statistics on American Politics 1999–2000*, Washington DC, CQ Press.

Starobin, P. (1994), 'Did God bless America?, *National Journal*, 26:50, 10 December, 2930.

Sutter, R. (1978), 'Immigrants and community', in J. M. Collier (ed.), *Forces in the Shaping of American Culture*, Los Alamitos, Hwong Publishing.

Truman, T. (1971), 'A critique of Seymour M. Lipset's article, "Value differences, absolute or relative: the english-speaking democracies", *Canadian Journal of Political Science/Revue Canadienne de Science Politique*, 4:4, December, 497–525.

Wiebe, R. H. (1995), *Self-Rule: A Cultural History of American History*, Chicago, University of Chicago Press.

Wilentz, S. (1984), 'Against exceptionalism: class consciousness and the American labor movement, 1790–1920', *International Labor and Working Class History*, 26, Autumn, 1–24.

Wilson, G. K. (1998), *Only in America? The Politics of the United States in Comparative Perspective*, Chatham, Chatham House Publishers.

Wright, J. W. (ed.) (2000), *The New York Times Almanac 2001*, New York, Penguin.

Wrobel, D. M. (1993), *The End of American Exceptionalism: Frontier Anxiety from the Old West to the New Deal*, Lawrence, University Press of Kansas.

Zolberg, A. Z. (1988), 'The roots of American exceptionalism', in J. Heffer and J. Rovet (eds), *Why is There No Socialism in the United States/Pourquoi N'y a-t-il pas de Socialisme aux Etats-Unis?*, Paris, Ecole des Hautes Etudes en Sciences Sociales, 101–18.

2

The American dream and the modern economy

The 'American dream' is a widely cited phrase. It suggests that the US is a **meritocratic** society in which individuals can become prosperous and climb the economic ladder through hard work, self-reliance and the adoption of entrepreneurial attitudes. It follows as a corollary that there is an element of personal responsibility and failure if they remain poor. Benjamin Franklin (1706–90) – one of the 'founding fathers' who wrote the US Constitution – has been widely seen as the personification of the 'dream'. His family could not afford to give him a college education and he became apprenticed as a printer. By the age of 42 he had made a fortune in the printing trade and subsequently as a publisher, allowing him to turn his attention to interests such as science and politics. Franklin believed that others could follow in his footsteps, and his autobiography offered advice to intending immigrants: 'If they are poor, they begin first as Servants or Journeymen; and if they are sober, industrious, and frugal, they soon become Masters, establish themselves in Business, marry, raise Families, and become respectable Citizens' (quoted in Bellah *et al.* 1985: 33).

As the nineteenth century progressed, American popular culture celebrated the upward mobility and progress of the self-made individual. Horatio Alger, an influential novelist, wrote *Ragged Dick, or Street Life in New York with the Bootblacks* (1867–68) and countless other stories in which the hero escapes poverty through effort and hard work. Even Karl Marx – the founding father of communism – acknowledged that, in the US, there was considerable movement up and down the income ladder: 'Classes are not yet fixed, but in continual flux, with a persistent interchange of their elements' (quoted in Kingston 2000: 60).

The dream is tied to theories of economic individualism. These rest upon a belief in the free market and the unfettered right of individuals to buy and sell both goods and services – including their own labour – as they choose. Two beliefs are axiomatic:

- Individuals should be self-reliant. They have a responsibility to provide for themselves and their families. They should not look to, or depend upon government provision.
- The role of government should be confined to functions such as national security, the upholding of the law and the preservation of order (often described as **laissez-faire** or free-market economics). From this perspective, government attempts to interfere with the interplay of supply and demand, or constrain self-interest, will lead only to the mismanagement and the misallocation of resources. Unrestrained, however, the market will generate economic growth and expansion.

Some have represented the dream – and the free market theories upon which it is structured – as an illusion. However, it has roots in the realities of early America. In Europe, land was held either by a small class of owners or divided into small, peasant plots. However, the American continent had, as Franklin remarked, a strikingly different character: 'Land being . . . Plenty in America, and so cheap as that a labouring Man, who understands Husbandry, can in a short Time save Money enough to purchase a Piece of new Land sufficient for a Plantation' (quoted in Greene 1993: 98).

The opening up of the western 'frontier' offered further opportunities to later immigrants. Although, to an extent, it merely confirmed existing realities of land acquisition, the 1862 Homestead Act allowed settlers to gain the legal ownership of 160 acres of land once they had been resident for five years and had paid nominal registration fees. A generation later, compulsory public schooling enabled immigrant children to learn English, acquire basic skills and gain employment. In 1940 the education system was hailed by the president of Harvard University, James Bryant Conant, as a 'vast engine' for 'regaining that great gift to each succeeding generation – opportunity, a gift that was once the promise of the frontier' (Sawhill and McMurrer 1996c). Others argue that the opportunities for economic mobility rested upon the laissez-faire and deregulated character of the American economy. This, they assert, created large numbers of entry-level jobs in the labour market and allowed incoming immigrants to acquire funds and establish small businesses. From these beginnings, it is said, significant numbers became prosperous.

Nonetheless, the traditional picture of the American dream should be placed in context and qualified. Although the idea of the dream has been important, there are reasons for doubting its veracity as a description of the American experience. First, those who portray the US as a 'land of opportunity' do not always acknowledge that some groupings faced institutional barriers that systematically denied them opportunities. African-Americans, in particular, faced *de jure* segregation (known as the Jim Crow laws) in the southern states and *de facto* segregation in the North. They were confined to the unskilled labour market or – in a few cases – small-scale and under-capitalised entrepreneurship within the black neighbourhoods. Others were held back by social barriers. Few women, for example, succeeded as entrepreneurs. Furthermore, in many of the white ethnic and Catholic communities – such as those drawn from Eastern and Southern Europe – family loyalties and neighbourhood obligations were seen as pivotal. The unrestrained pursuit of wealth was represented as an abandonment of these ties. In addition, inherited class distinctions were not altogether absent in American society. Particular preparatory schools, the Ivy League universities and some country clubs had a quasi-aristocratic ethos. Furthermore, families such as the Rockefellers and Gettys became synonymous with inherited wealth.

Since the nineteenth century, the opportunities for small-scale entrepreneurship have been progressively closed off. Liberals such as John Dewey (1859–1952) attributed this to the process of industrial concentration and monopolisation. He argued that the prescribed virtues of hard work, dedication and effort no longer brought forth reward. Those on the conservative Right draw similar conclusions but emphasise the growth of 'big government', the increasing regulation of economic activity, and the erosion of laissez-faire. They point, in particular, to the reining in of traditional individualism during the Progressive era at the beginning of the twentieth century, a process built upon by the New Deal and the Great Society programmes. Although Herbert Croly, whose book *The Promise of American Life* (1989) underpinned Progressivism, presented his ideas as a realisation of individualism, much of his thinking pointed in another direction. He argued that the scale and complexity of twentieth-century economic life required government interventionism and the construction of large-scale, national forms of organisation.

The dream has also been subject to another form of criticism. Some have questioned whether it provides a proper moral basis for American society. They suggest that it confines individuals to economic goals and purposes, thereby denying them other forms of the experience. Benjamin Franklin is said to have been 'incapable of dreaming, or doubting, of being mystified' (quoted in Nuechterlein 2000). Christopher Lasch, a communitarian theorist, argued

---

The American dream and self-interest

Those who endorse the principles of economic individualism suggest that it provides the most effective basis for the social order because it harnesses self-interest. In his reports on the early American republic, Jean Hector St John de Crevecoeur represented this as the foundation of the dream and the essence of American identity: 'Here the rewards of his industry follow with equal steps the progress of his labour; his labour is founded on the basis of nature, self-interest; can it want a stronger allurement? . . . From involuntary idleness, servile dependence, penury, and useless labour, he has passed to toils of a very different nature, rewarded by ample subsistence. This is an American' (Crevecoeur 1986: 70).

that the dream displaced another, and much more profound understanding of individual and social progress. In the early and mid-nineteenth century, he suggested there were hopes that a republican society could be built. Large numbers would be property holders and, although there would be economic inequalities, rigid class distinctions would be absent. All would participate in civic affairs and the process of government. Such a society would offer more – at least for its white citizens – than mere material reward. Individuals could move beyond the world of work and develop their intellectual and aesthetic abilities. The original ideal, Lasch asserts: 'was nothing less than a classless society, understood to mean not only the absence of hereditary privilege and legally recognized distinctions of rank but a refusal to tolerate the separation of learning and labor' (Lasch 1995: 64).

The American dream today

Despite doubts about the extent to which the dream captured the realities of American history, and the questions about its legitimacy, it still has a hold on the popular imagination. The dream was, for example, cited by former president, Bill Clinton: 'The American dream that we were all raised on is a simple but powerful one – if you work hard and play by the rules you should be given a chance to go as far as your God-given ability will take you' (quoted in Hochschild 1995: 18). Large numbers believe that American society still offers these opportunities. In 1983–87 the General Social Survey asked 1,420 respondents to identify the prerequisites of personal achievement. It presented the statement: 'America has an open society. What one achieves in life no longer depends on one's family background, but on the abilities one has and the education one acquires.' In reply, 40.3 per cent 'strongly agreed'; 44.7 per cent 'somewhat agreed'; 13.4 per cent 'somewhat disagreed'; and 1.6 per cent 'strongly disagreed' (General Social Survey 2001).

Other studies draw similar conclusions. When asked in 1990 whether success depended upon hard work or 'luck and connections', 44 per cent of Americans compared with 24 per cent of the British and 22 per cent of the French pointed to the former (Lipset 1997: 81–2). A 1994 study revealed that 74 per cent of those asked agreed with the statement that 'In America, if you work hard, you can be anything you want to be' (Lipset 1997: 287). This belief thrives, in particular, among recent immigrants who draw on comparisons between the US and their country of origin (Mahler 1995: 233).

There is some empirical confirmation for these sentiments, particularly when **intragenerational** income mobility is considered. The US Treasury used data drawn from income tax returns between 1979 and 1988 that showed that 86 per cent of tax-paying households who were in the lowest **quintile** – or fifth of the population – in 1979 had moved upwards by 1988 (Sawhill and McMurrer 1996a). Similarly, using data collected by the University of

Michigan's Panel Survey on Income Distribution, W. Michael Cox and Richard Alm compared the economic status of the same individuals in both 1975 and 1991. Their findings are recorded in Table 2.1. They show what happened in later years to those who were in the five different income quintiles in 1975. For example, 14.6 per cent who were in the lowest quintile in 1975 had, by 1991, progressed to the second lowest quintile. Although Cox and Alm's study is confined to earnings levels and does not consider the extent to which individuals were able to gain different types of occupation, it does reveal that an overwhelming majority of those in the sample climbed the income ladder. As they note, only 5 per cent of those in the lowest quintile in 1975 remained there in 1991. 'Where did they end up? A majority made it to the top three fifths of the income distribution – middle class or better. Most amazing of all, almost three out of ten of the low-income earners from 1975 had risen to the uppermost 20 percent by 1991. More than three-quarters found their way into the highest tiers of income earners for at least one year by 1991' (Cox and Alm 1999: 73).

Table 2.1 *Income mobility, 1975–91 (percentage in each quintile)*

	Lowest 1991	Second 1991	Third 1991	Fourth 1991	Highest 1991
Lowest 1975	5.1	14.6	21.0	30.3	29.0
Second 1975	4.2	23.5	20.3	25.2	26.8
Third 1975	3.3	19.3	28.3	30.1	19.0
Fourth 1975	1.9	9.3	18.8	32.6	37.4
Highest 1975	0.9	2.8	10.2	23.6	62.5

Source: adapted from Cox and Alm 1999:73.

Cox and Alm attribute these shifts to a range of variables. Echoing some of Benjamin Franklin's prescriptions written 200 years earlier, they emphasise the importance of educational qualifications, thrift, an acceptance of family responsibilities and personal resilience. However, they add to this by also stressing the role of contemporary virtues. These include the importance of computer literacy, a willingness to move between regions and a readiness to acquire new skills through retraining programmes (Cox and Alm 1999: 85–7).

Some studies of **intergenerational** mobility – which record the extent to which an individual has a significantly different occupation to that of his or her parent – also sound an optimistic note. Featherman and Hauser's 1978 study of men showed that among those in the upper non-manual grouping, the highest of the categories they used, only 29.3 per cent had a father who was similarly placed. Significant numbers had been drawn into the upper non-manual group from the families of manual and farm workers. These findings lead Paul W. Kingston to conclude that 'working-class sons commonly became middle class themselves' (Kingston 2000: 66–7). In other words, the effects of family status on their children's eventual occupation appear to have lessened.

Some dub this the declining importance of class. The process has, in significant part, been attributed to the growing proportion of those from low-income families who have gained college degrees.

However, much of this data can be approached differently. Featherman and Hauser's study also shows that large numbers remained within the grouping into which they were born. Amongst those born into upper non-manual families, 70.8 per cent stayed within non-manual occupations (Kingston 2000: 66). Furthermore, the increase in educational opportunity – and the declining importance of class – was offset by a decline in other forms of mobility (see pp. 39–40). While this leads some observers to conclude that overall upward mobility rates remained broadly stable during the last three decades of the twentieth century, others assert that the rate of mobility dropped back during the late 1970s and 1980s (Sawhill and McMurrer 1996b). Steven Rytina, for example, argues in his study of education and mobility: 'It is an exaggeration to say that rank begets rank without meritocratic qualification, but much less of one than a generation ago' (Rytina 2000: 1270). It has, furthermore, been suggested that the slowdown in rates of mobility has had particular consequences for those groupings that were already subject to lower rates of upward mobility. A study of earnings between 1967 and 1991 reported that women, African-Americans and those with few skills or qualifications were most likely to remain in the bottom income quintile of the population (see Table 2.2). At the same time, they were also the least likely to remain – if they reached it – in the top income quintile (Gittleman and Joyce 1995: 6–7).

Table 2.2   *Sex and race differences in mobility, 1990–91 (percentage remaining within earnings quintile)*

	Lowest quintile	Highest quintile
White men	56	77
Black men	65	54
White women	73	66
Black women	73	42

Note: The figures are for year-round, full-time workers.
Source: Adapted from Gittleman and Joyce 1995:6.

Furthermore, most comparisons with other nations suggest that the US is not – despite the American dream – exceptional. In 1959 Seymour Martin Lipset and Rheinhard Bendix concluded there was relatively little difference in intergenerational mobility rates across nine industrialised countries. In a later study, Alan Kerckoff, Richard Campbell and Idee Winfield-Laird argued that although there were differences between the US and Britain, they were not rooted in the character of American society and culture: 'They find that more individuals in the United States move up in the occupational hierarchy than move up in Britain, but ultimately conclude that this difference is explained by differences in economic growth, not by differences in the social structures that determine opportunity and achievement in each country' (McMurrer, Condon and Sawhill 1997).

Why is mobility limited?

Benjamin Franklin suggested that upward mobility depended upon personal virtues such as frugality and thrift. In practice, although variables such as a willingness to take advantage of educational opportunities play an important role, the rate of mobility depends, to a significant extent, on long-term change in the character of the economic process and, in particular, on the occupational structure. Studies therefore refer to this as **structural mobility**.

For much of the twentieth century the US economy grew at a rapid rate. The numbers required on the land contracted, while the industrial and commercial sectors demanded increasing quantities of labour. At the same time, the proportion of the overall workforce in manual occupations fell while, correspondingly, the percentage of non-manual or 'white-collar' workers rose. Between 1910 and 1940, for example, the number of non-manual jobs grew by 73 per cent (Lipset and Bendix 1959:150). These changes – which were tied to rising productivity levels allowing more efficient and less labour-intensive forms of production – provided the basis for high levels of intragenerational and intergenerational mobility.

The contraction in rates of mobility towards the end of the twentieth century can be tied to the slowdown in overall rates of economic expansion and productivity growth during the 1970s. The economy continued to expand, except in the recessions in the early 1980s and 1990s, but at a more lacklustre pace. Similarly, between the early 1970s and mid-1990s, productivity growth averaged about 1.4 per cent annually, about half that achieved during the preceding period. There were, consequently, lower levels of mobility and a solidification of existing socio-economic rankings (Gilbert and Kahl 1992: 153).

There are other reasons why individuals tend to stay within their grouping of origin or, if they do shift upwards or downwards, mobility only has a short-range character. Some point to the character of public schooling, particularly in the inner-city neighbourhoods. As a Wall Street security guard told an interviewer:

> My seven-year-old son is in the second grade at the local public school. It's completely underfunded and lacking resources, and most of the kids are from teenage mothers with fathers in jail. My children have been put in a position where they will not be able to compete . . . How do you think that makes me feel? Trapped. That the American dream ended with my generation. (Cohen 2001: 33)

Cultural factors also play a role. Children acquire the attitudes and values of their parents and peers through the socialisation process. Aspirations and expectations are passed from generation to generation. Studies suggest that those on the higher rungs of the occupational ladder 'transmit' values such as the ability to wait for rewards – known as **deferred gratification**. Through both conscious and unconscious forms of parenting, they ensure that their children have assertive personalities and can lead independent lives. All of this increases the likelihood that occupational categories will be reproduced in successor generations.

However, both liberals and conservatives suggest other reasons why upward mobility – the core of the American dream – proved increasingly elusive as the twentieth century progressed. The liberal critique emphasises four factors.

- Racial and ethnic minorities – and women – have encountered systematic discrimination. For years, segregation and rigid employment rules ensured that senior posts in almost all occupations were the preserve of white men. Today, some observers – particularly those associated with liberalism and feminism – suggest that overt discrimination has been displaced by the 'glass ceiling' (see p. 42).
- The process of economic concentration and the increasing hold of monopolies over the American economy – have closed off market opportunities to those seeking to build their own businesses. Few can compete with giant corporations such as McDonald's or Microsoft. Many liberals support antitrust legislation and attempts to break up companies that have a monopolistic hold over particular markets.
- The fate of those who are self-employed and the success of small-scale business projects is dependent upon access to loan capital. The banking system, liberals argue, has been reluctant to lend to women, the minorities, and those living in poor neighbourhoods.
- Some talk in terms of an 'hourglass economy'. The labour market is divided into two distinct and separate sectors, and there is little movement between them. The primary market is structured around highly paid forms of employment, job security, regulated working conditions and the application of due process in the imposition of rules and in promotion procedures. In contrast, the secondary labour market rests on poor wage levels, temporary and often insecure employment, and arbitrary job structures. Many people living in the poorer neighbourhoods are confined to the secondary market because of poor qualifications and a lack of knowledge about job opportunities.

For their part, conservatives stress other considerations. They maintain that the American dream rested on an individual's own ambition and effort. It was fostered by the principle of self-reliance that governed the early American republic. However, conservatives argue, the growth of government has stifled individual initiative and created a dependency culture. High taxation levels have reduced the rewards offered to those who work hard or venture into entrepreneurship. Government assistance programmes have discouraged some from finding employment and affirmative action has allowed some to climb the occupational ladder when it has been ill-deserved.

In some sectors of the economy, there has also been a process of 'producer capture'. This occurs when particular groups use their influence with political decision makers to secure and maintain a privileged economic position for themselves by excluding competitors from the market. In 1937 the New York taxi drivers persuaded the city authorities to impose a limit on the number of licensed cabs in the city. This form of regulation restricted competition and thereby ensured that fares could be maintained at particular levels. It also prevented entry to the market by those for whom it could be a first step towards a stable livelihood.

Finally, conservatives also claim that although there are success stories, many in the racial and ethnic minorities have not adjusted to the requirements of the modern economy. Indeed, some minority cultures are described as dysfunctional. Significant numbers of young black men, it is said, have turned to crime and gang-based activities. While white males have – measured at the time of birth – a 4.4 per cent chance of serving a term of imprisonment at some point in their lives; the corresponding figure for black males is 28.5 per cent (Wright 2000: 312).

Labour union membership

Chapter 1 recorded the historical weakness of the American labour movement. Despite periods of militancy, membership was limited to a relatively small proportion of the overall workforce. The proportion fell still further during the 1980s and 1990s. This was partly because of the two recessions and the decline of traditional industries.

Table 2.3   *Percentage of workers in a labour union, 1985–99*

	All workers	Private sector workers	Public sector workers
1985	18	14.3	35.7
1990	16.1	11.9	36.5
1995	14.9	10.3	37.7
1999	13.9	9.4	37.3

Note: Although these are the membership figures, a higher proportion of the workforce is covered by union agreements.
Source: Adapted from US Census Bureau 2000:445.

Class rigidities

All observers accept that there is an unequal distribution of income and wealth in the US. However, those who have faith in the American dream – and the belief that significant numbers have the opportunity to join the wealthiest classes – deny the social and political importance of these disparities. As Steven Rytina puts it: 'Mobility implies that the hurts of inequality are potentially fleeting' (Rytina 2000: 1227). Liberal and radical commentators do not, however, believe that American society has realised the aspirations associated with the dream. They conclude that mobility has only a limited and short-range character and that, therefore, economic inequality is of much greater significance. They emphasise the scale and extent to which income and wealth are unequally distributed and stress the degree to which an individual's life chances are determined by initial socio-economic status, race and gender.

Income and wealth

Income refers to the flow of money to a household. It includes wages, salaries, interest from savings and other earnings. The term 'wealth' refers to a household's total assets. In contrast with the flow of income, it is a **stock**. A household's wealth will include **equity** in a house – the difference between its market value and the sum still owed – as well as stocks and shares, cars and a range of consumer durables.

The distribution of income

Statistics compiled by the US Census Bureau, which divide the population into quintiles on the basis of income, show that the richest fifth of the population gains almost half the country's income (US Census Bureau 2001a). Correspondingly, the poorest fifth receive only 3.7 per cent. Furthermore, although median household income rose to the highest ever level during the boom years of the mid and late 1990s, the degree of inequality increased. The share of aggregate income received by income quintiles, by household, in 2000 was: lowest 3.6 per cent; second 8.9 per cent; third 14.8 per cent; fourth 23 per cent; and highest 49.6 per cent.

Some groupings are disproportionately concentrated on the lower rungs of the income ladder while, conversely, others have higher levels of median income. Gender, race and ethnicity play a particular role.

Gender

Women's income continues to lag behind that of men. In 1999 women's average hourly wages were 84 per cent of male hourly earnings (National Center for Policy Analysis 2000a). Furthermore, as a 1995 report concluded, only 5 per cent of senior managers at *Fortune* 1000 industrial and *Fortune* 500 service companies were women. These disparities have been described in different ways. Some talk of a 'gender gap'. Others refer to the 'pink ghetto' or talk of a 'glass ceiling', defined by the *Wall Street Journal* as the 'invisible but impenetrable barrier between women and the executive suite' (quoted in Furchtgott-Roth and Stolba 1999: 18). How should these disparities be explained?

The occupational and promotional barriers that constitute the 'ceiling' are, it has been argued, largely attributable to prejudice and discrimination by white male managers. Those associated with liberalism and feminism call – on this basis – for the adoption of affirmative action programmes. In their most modest form, these involve seeking out job applicants from women and minorities. However, some also call for 'quotas' so that preference is given – when making appointments – to those other than white males.

Diana Furchtgott-Roth and Christine Stolba adopt a different perspective. They suggest that nearly all the differences between male and female earnings – and their respective places on the career ladder – can be attributed to variables other than discrimination (Furchtgott-Roth and Stolba 1999: xvii). Women, they argue, often have fewer opportunities for promotion because they have chosen to work on a part-time basis or have spent a number of years away from work while their children were young. Women have also often followed different career paths to men. Many study different subjects at college. For example, although women now earn over half all the BA and MA degrees that are awarded, they are under-represented in subjects such as mathematics and computer science that may lead to the most high-paying forms of employment. As a consequence, they work in less well-remunerated occupations. In addition, women choose part-time jobs or posts that offer job flexibility so that they can balance out the work and family needs.

These choices, conservative commentators suggest, reflect personal decisions by women rather than discrimination. As Elizabeth Fox-Genovese has argued: 'Even highly successful women frequently want to spend much more time with their young children than the sixty-hour weeks required by the corporate fast tracks will permit' (quoted in Furchtgott-Roth and Stolba 1999: 17).

Nonetheless, despite this, women are likely to make significant occupational and income gains over the coming decades. Both the service and financial sectors, where women are relatively well represented at managerial level, are likely to grow (Furchtgott-Roth and Stolba 1999: xix).

Race and ethnicity

There are also significant racial and ethnic disparities. Although segregation – which confined almost all blacks in the southern states to manual forms of labour – ended in the 1960s, African-Americans and Latinos are still concentrated in low-wage employment. This affects more than income. These types of jobs offer fewer fringe benefits and significantly less access to health insurance and pension schemes. There are four principal reasons why many from the minorities are 'locked' into these sectors of the labour market.

First, they have fewer marketable skills and were less successful at school and in college. Those who have comparable educational and professional

African-Americans and the American dream

The American dream does not only have a hold among those who have gained material success. Jennifer Hochschild suggests that even low-income African-Americans share its essential tenets. Indeed, they have greater faith in the dream than the black middle class. Paradoxically, middle class income and status has risen very significantly since the segregationist era came to a close in the 1960s. Nonetheless, Hochschild argues, the adherence of low-income blacks to the dream may be undermined by material circumstances in the urban neighbourhoods. This will have significant social and political consequences:

> But any nightly newscast suggests how fragile that continued commitment is for those subject to drive-by shootings and schools innocent of plumbing, let alone textbooks. Thus if middle class African Americans may lead other Americans into disillusionment with the ideology despite their success, so a few poor African-Americans may, with even greater reason, lead other poor Americans into a rejection of the dream that will make affluent alienation seem trivial. (Hochschild 1995: 88)

qualifications have similar and, in some instances, higher levels of income. Although a relatively high proportion live in poverty, a significant proportion of Asian-Americans aged twenty-five and over have advanced qualifications and their median income is, in contrast with other minorities, higher than the national average.

Second, many within the minority communities rely on informal networks for information about job vacancies. This tradition reproduces labour market inequalities by limiting individuals to particular forms of employment (Fletcher 2000). Third, the processes of *deindustrialisation* and the relocation of businesses on the outskirts of cities created a mismatch. Disproportionate numbers from the minorities live in inner-city or suburban neighbourhoods where there are now only limited job opportunities.

Finally, some suggest that immigration has bloated the unskilled labour market, forcing down wage levels. In 1990 Frank Morris of Morgan State University told Congressional staff members:

> It is clear that America's black population is bearing a disproportionate share of immigrants' competition for jobs, housing and social services . . . Many of the immigrants compete directly with blacks in the same labor markets and occupations and have become substitutes for black workers more often than they have become complements . . . The pervasive effects of ethnic-network recruiting and the spread of non-English languages in the workplace has, in effect, locked many blacks out of occupations where they once dominated. (Quoted in Beck 1996: 227)

Table 2.4 *Median income by sex, race and Hispanic origin, 2000 (dollars)*

	White	Black	Asian	Hispanic	All races
Male	29,696	21,662	30,475	19,833	28,272
Female	16,218	16,081	17,314	12,255	16,190

Source: Adapted from US Census Bureau 2001b.

Most liberals condemn the scale of inequality in contemporary America and seek amelioration of the disparities through increased taxation and other forms of government interventionism. Conservatives see inequality in different terms. For many, it is a natural and inevitable characteristic of all societies. It is a function of demand and supply for particular skills and abilities. Furthermore, a number of conservatives point to the economic successes of the Asian-American communities. As Table 2.4 reveals, their median income exceeds that of whites. This, some on the Right suggest, is attributable to work, entrepreneurship and family life. A cultural shift by those in other groupings could, they assert, yield similar rewards.

The minimum wage

The US has a legal minimum wage, although there has always been an informal or 'black' economy resting on illegal immigrants and other undocumented aliens that pays considerably less. For liberals, the declining real value of the minimum wage is a further cause of inequality. Some conservatives suggest, however, that a legal minimum has created increased unemployment among low-skilled workers. Employers, it is said, will hire fewer workers if there is an artificially inflated wage rate.

Table 2.5   *The minimum wage, 1978–98 (constant 1998 dollars)*

1978	6.63
1980	6.13
1985	5.07
1990	4.74
1995	4.55
1998	5.15

Source: Adapted from US Census Bureau 2000:439.

Wealth

Wealth – or asset ownership – is also unequally distributed. Table 2.6 shows the net worth of different households. This records household wealth once debts have been taken into account. In some instances debts exceed assets and a

Table 2.6   Percentage distribution of household net worth, 1995

	Zero or negative	$1 to $4,999	$5,000 to $9,999	$10,000 to $24,999	$25,000 to $49,999	$50,000 to $99,999	$100,000 to $249,999	$250,000 to $499,999	$500,000 and over
White	8.8	12.5	6.0	11.3	11.7	16.8	21.1	7.9	4.0
Black	21.7	24.7	6.8	13.9	12.6	14.0	5.5	0.6	0.2
Hispanic	17.8	28.3	9.0	12.9	9.9	10.7	8.6	2.4	0.5

Source: Adapted from US Census Bureau 2001c.

household's net worth is therefore a negative figure. In many other cases, households will have few assets apart from the equity in their house. There are again some stark differences between the races. In over a fifth of African-American households the debts are greater than the assets. Although blacks are increasingly well represented in the middle categories, only a small handful of African-Americans can be found among the richest Americans.

Furthermore, the distribution of wealth became more unequal during the final decades of the twentieth century. This was partly because – under the Reagan administration – the taxation system became less progressive and allowed the higher income groupings to retain a greater proportion of their income. Corporate and inheritance taxes were reduced, while the top rate of income tax was cut from 70 per cent to 28 per cent. At the same time, there were substantial stock market gains for investors (Gilbert and Kahl 1992: 104–8).

Underclass and 'overclass'

Despite the disparities of income and wealth, most commentaries are reluctant to emphasise class divisions. Instead, almost all people in regular forms of employment – whether it is manual or white-collar – are described as 'middle class'. Having said this, it has been increasingly widely recognised that there are some who are excluded from the ranks of the middle class. The 'underclass' entered the American vocabulary in the early 1980s. The word refers to those who are on the margins of the metropolitan labour force and 'locked' into sustained poverty. It is not, however, simply a synonym for those who are poor but, instead, also conveys a number of implicit assumptions.

> Although there is no consensus about how to define the underclass, these families are usually described as being headed by females who are permanently unemployed, persistently poor, dependent on welfare, giving birth out of wedlock, predominantly black or Hispanic, poorly educated, and living in blighted urban areas overwhelmed with crime, pollution, drugs, and other social problems. (Bryner 1998: 48–9)

The growth of the underclass has been attributed to different factors. In *Losing Ground*, Charles Murray argues that the scale of assistance offered by federal welfare provision – most notably Aid to Families with Dependent Children (AFDC) – had made single motherhood a viable proposition and encouraged individuals not to take low-paid employment (Murray 1984: 154–66). In contrast with conservative commentators who, like Murray, concentrate on the character of financial assistance to the poor, William Julius Wilson emphasises the economic and social isolation of the urban poor. Desegregation allowed the black middle classes to move away while the black poor remained in the central city neighbourhoods. Furthermore, most job growth has been concentrated in the suburbs, contributing to increased unemployment in the cities (Massey and Denton 1993: 143).

However, although the word 'underclass' is widely used – and the fears it inspired led to welfare reform in 1996 – the concept does present difficulties. First, the most usual representations of the underclass suggest that is a culturally distinct grouping, structured around the young unmarried black mother and the single black male. It evokes images of drug abuse, violence and alienation. There is, however, little evidence that cultural values among the poor and long-term unemployed differ markedly from those of the American mainstream.

The use of the collective term 'underclass' also obscures the differences among the urban poor. At the beginning of the 1980s, Ken Auletta distinguished between four groupings. There were, he asserted, significant differences between those he called the traumatized (who were 'drunks, drifters, homeless shopping-bag ladies and released mental patients'), violent street criminals, nonviolent hustlers (many of whom were tied to the underground economy) and long-term welfare recipients (Kingston 2000: 177).

Some – particularly liberals and radicals – reject the notion of an underclass altogether. They concentrate on the impact of particular social problems such as homelessness, and draw a contrast between government provision for the poor in Western Europe and that in the US. In a 1994 study, Christopher Jencks estimates that the American homeless population was about 400,000. He attributes the numbers living on the streets to the absence of a welfare state and 'collective indifference' (quoted in Perry and Perry 2000: 157–8).

There has also been some consideration of those at the other end of the economic scale. The word 'overclass' was first used by Gunnar Myrdal, a Swedish sociologist who undertook a pioneering study of African-American life. In the 1990s the term was resurrected by Michael Lind, a journalist and commentator. Lind argues that the 'overclass' refers to about 5 or 10 per cent of the population. It is: '. . . the credentialized managerial-professional elite, consisting of Americans with advanced degrees . . . and their spouses and children . . . its members provide the overwhelming majority of leaders in the highest reaches of American business, politics, education, and journalism' (Lind 1996: 34).

The overclass – which is largely, although not exclusively white, lives in gated communities – which are private estates offering privacy and security – or the more exclusive suburbs. Like the underclass, the overclass has a quasi-hereditary character. It is not a meritocracy, open to all who climb the economic ladder. Instead, although there is some mobility, those born into the ranks of the overclass will almost certainly maintain their position and bequeath it to their own children.

Lind argues that those in the overclass have a number of distinctive attitudes – based upon their own self-interest – towards public policy issues. Their employment of nannies and maids, many of whom are from the Caribbean or

Latin America, leads them to support open immigration. Although they lean towards cultural liberalism, they are hostile towards trade unionism, high taxation and the provision of federal assistance programmes for the poor (Lind 1996: 37–44).

Insured and uninsured

Significant numbers of Americans have difficulties – or may face difficulties – when they fall ill. In the absence of a welfare state, access to health provision can be haphazard. Individuals are usually dependent upon private insurance, often provided for full-time workers by employers, Medicaid, a system of basic health provision for the poor administered by the states, and Medicare, a contributory programme for senior citizens.

Studies conducted in 1994–95 suggested that almost a quarter of the pre-retirement population lacked full health insurance: 22.4 per cent were uninsured for at least one month and 7.4 per cent were uninsured for the entire period (National Center for Policy Analysis 2001). Furthermore, those who have insurance may not be covered for all eventualities or all forms of ill-health. In 1995 17 million insured adults reported difficulties in obtaining medical care or in paying for it. Although the number of employers offering insurance coverage rose during the late 1990s as the labour market tightened, it fell in 2000. This reflected the economic slowdown and the rising costs of health care. Latinos face particular difficulties. One report suggested that 32 per cent were uninsured (Pear 2001).

The 'new economy' of the 1990s

Although the 1990s began amidst recession, unemployment and claims that the US faced deeply rooted difficulties, this gave way to profound optimism. The new mood was fuelled by sustained economic growth that, in the first quarter of 1998 reached an annualised rate of 6.1 per cent and, at the end of 1999, hit 8.3 per cent. Despite the early years, the US economy created almost 22 million new jobs over the course of the decade (*The Economist* 2000: 49). By the end of 1999, unemployment had fallen to 4.1 per cent, below the level that many economists had predicted would trigger increased inflation. However, inflation persistently refused to rise. In 1997 the Consumer Price Index increased by only 1.7 per cent. Furthermore, as a consequence of the economic boom, earlier fears that the federal government budget deficit could never be eliminated proved groundless. The budget moved out of deficit in 1998 – largely because tax revenues increase during periods of prosperity – and a surplus of $148 billion was projected for 2002 (Alsop 1998: 104).

Against this background, there were assertions that individuals could again hope to realise the American dream and there were opportunities awaiting those with entrepreneurial skills. Furthermore, it was said, the 'new economy' had overcome the dangers traditionally faced by Western economies, particularly the threats posed by 'overheating' (excessive consumer demand levels that lead to inflation) and recession (which brings unemployment in its wake). This led some to talk of a 'new' or 'Goldilocks economy'. Like the porridge in the fable, the US economy appeared to be neither too 'hot' nor too 'cold'. The 1990s boom and the emergence of the 'new economy' can be attributed to six factors.

- Productivity – the amount of goods and services produced in an hour of work – allows companies to produce on a more efficient basis. With productivity growth, firms can avert price rises and, at the same time, increase the wages paid to their employees. Between 1972 and 1995 US productivity grew only slowly, at an annual rate of about 1.5 per cent. From then onwards, there was a significant rise to 2.6 per cent (Bartlett 2001). This was largely attributed to the computer revolution, the internet and the growth of the 'dot.com' sector of the economy.
- There was intensified competition, forcing companies to keep price rises to a minimum. Deregulation reduced the barriers to entry in a number of markets such as transportation and energy supply. New firms could enter markets where, previously, small numbers of companies had a stranglehold. New technology also played a role. Some web-based ventures were, for example, launched with very little capital.
- The weakness of the trades unions and the limited character of the American 'welfare state' led to a low NAIRU (Non-Accelerating Inflation Rate of Unemployment). Even when in 1997 unemployment fell to below 5 per cent, traditionally a strong bargain position, workers did not insist upon wage rises that would have led to subsequent increases in prices.
- The US economy is now less dependent on oil, making it more resistant to the 'supply-side shocks' that arose in earlier decades as a consequence of turmoil in the Middle-East or significant increases in the world price of oil.
- American companies are much more exposed to competitive pressures for another reason. The process of globalisation has begun to reshape the American economy. Trade barriers – such as tariffs and quotas – which formerly sheltered some industries, have been lowered. The end of the Cold War opened up new markets and freed up resources for non-military purposes. Furthermore, the combined value of American imports and exports now amounts to about a quarter of the country's Gross Domestic Product (GDP). The figure is twice that of a generation ago (Tuxeira and Rogers 2000: 8).
- As the 1990s progressed, the upturn gained momentum. Increasing disposable income – and a degree of deregulation – led an increasing proportion of the American population to buy company shares. Share ownership – once the preserve of a privileged few – became much more widely dispersed. As

shares increased in market value, people felt more prosperous. Their spending led to a rise in overall consumption – a process known as the **wealth effect** – fuelling the boom still further.

The emergence of the 'new economy' had important consequences. Although, as Table 2.7 illustrates, there were still significant ethnic and racial disparities, per capita income grew as the decade progressed, particularly after 1995.

Table 2.7   *Income, race and ethnicity, 1990–99 (per capita median income, constant 1999 dollars)*

	All races	White	Black	Hispanic
1990	18,339	19,458	11,494	10,738
1995	18,832	20,009	12,005	10,167
1996	19,257	20,367	12,635	10,669
1997	19,972	21,201	12,820	11,182
1998	20,564	21,867	13,243	11,687
1999	21,181	22,375	14,397	11,621

Source: Adapted from Wright 2001:323.

Second, as Table 2.8 shows, poverty levels dropped significantly. Indeed, by 2000, they had fallen to 11.3 per cent, the lowest figure since 1979, and only just above the lowest poverty rate that has been recorded, (11.1 per cent in 1973) (Seelye 2001). The poverty threshold is the basic minimum required so as to sustain an acceptable standard of living. It is adjusted annually and varies on the basis of the numbers of dependents living in the household. It does not, however, include non-cash benefits such as food stamps, Medicaid and housing provision.

Table 2.8   *Poverty, race and ethnicity, 1990–2000 (percentage of people living below the poverty level)*

	All races	White	Black	Hispanic
1990	13.5	10.7	31.9	28.1
1995	13.8	11.2	29.3	30.3
1996	13.7	11.2	28.4	29.4
1997	13.3	11.0	26.5	27.1
1998	12.7	10.5	26.1	25.6
1999	11.8	9.8	23.6	22.8
2000	11.3	9.4	22.1	21.2

Source: Adapted from Wright 2001:323.

Alongside these changes, there were suggestions of a parallel shift. During the 1980s and early 1990s, it was argued, the pursuit of profit led to corporate downsizing and plant closures. This created severe social dislocation, particularly in cities across the Northeast. Large companies – such as General Motors in Flint, Michigan, which was the subject of Michael Moore's 1989 film, *Roger and Me* – appeared self-interested and soulless. However by 2000, some observers argued, pension funds and mutual funds owned the majority of shares in US companies. Increasingly, therefore, corporate strategists were being compelled to consider long-term performance – and the interests of their employees whose pensions are invested – rather than short-term results and a separate class of shareholders (Drucker 2001: 20).

Table 2.9   *Median household income, 1970–2000 (constant 2000 dollars)*

1970	33,746
1975	33,489
1980	35,238
1985	36,246
1990	38,446
1995	38,262
2000	42,148

Source: Adapted from US Census Bureau 2001d.

And the old economy

However, despite the confident assertions of those who talked of a 'new economy', others questioned whether there had been a lasting and fundamental shift in the character of the American economy. As the new millennium began, the US seemed – despite successive interest rate cuts – to be teetering on the edge of a recession. Economic growth slowed and almost came to a halt. At the same time, share prices – particularly in the dot.com sector – fell back. Increasingly, the 1990s boom was being represented as simply a cyclical upswing that would inevitably be followed by a prolonged downswing. The pessimists pointed to the economic weaknesses that underlay the boom and to the many features of the 'old economy' that still remained in place. For example, once memories of the 1990–1 recession faded, consumer confidence began to recover. Increasing numbers took out loans or borrowed on a credit card. Consumer indebtedness – a figure that excludes mortgages – doubled from $789.3 billion in 1990 to $1,395.4 billion in 1999 (Wright 2000: 326). Evidence from the late 1970s and early 1980s suggests that American families begin to reduce their overall spending once debt reaches about 7 per cent of their net financial assets (Cox and Alm 1999: 13). This could, in turn, lead producers and retailers to cut back production and investment.

As noted above, the wealth effect contributed to the consumer boom. However, correspondingly, as share values fell, households began to think again about their spending patterns. This had **deflationary** consequences for the entire economy. Moreover, although – as Table 2.9 shows – real income levels rose during the latter half of the 1990s, they were still, in 1995, only about 10 per cent higher than in the late 1970s. The long-term growth rate was therefore low and there were some significant falls during the intervening years. Furthermore, income levels dropped at the beginning of the new century. While the gap between blacks and whites narrowed, real median household income fell between 1999 and 2000 (Seelye 2001).

There are also important differences between the states. Despite economic growth in cities such as Atlanta, the South continues to lag behind the other regions. In 2000 per capita personal income was highest – at $40,640 – in Connecticut. Income levels in Mississippi – the poorest of the fifty states – were half that figure ($20,993) (Wright 2001: 321). Furthermore, the

---

Welfare

Welfare provision – for those with dependent children – became a federal **entitlement** in the 1930s. From then onwards, the numbers claiming welfare – principally single mothers – grew rapidly. It also provoked political controversy. Conservatives, in particular, argued that welfare payments, and other forms of assistance such as food stamps, had created a culture of dependency. Recipients no longer sought employment. Furthermore, there was no incentive to form stable family relationships. Against this background, there were proposals for reform. However, it took the election of a Republican majority in both houses of Congress to enact fundamental legislative change.

The August 1996 Personal Responsibility and Work Opportunity Act introduced Temporary Aid to Needy Families (TANF). Under TANF, assistance is limited to a maximum of five years during an individual's lifetime, although some states have restricted provision to as little as twenty-one months. No able-bodied adult can receive assistance for more than a two-year period at any one time. Furthermore, states can choose to deny welfare to unwed parents under eighteen and those who had further children while on welfare. Many who were formerly welfare recipients joined the labour market.

The Act was subsequently hailed as a success. The welfare rolls fell and there are indications that the number of out-of-wedlock births has dropped. The employment rate among single mothers – which had been 59 per cent in 1994 – rose to 74 per cent in 2001. Furthermore, their median real wage rose at an annualised rate of 3.1 per cent from 1996 onwards (Urban Institute 2001: 1). However, much of this may be attributable to the buoyancy of the economy during the latter half of the economy. Furthermore, the individual states may still have to make provision – under the guise of employment training – for the core of long-term welfare recipients who still have not found work once their five-year lifetime assistance has been exhausted.

uncertainties of a deregulated labour market created considerable job insecurity, even during a period of growth and relative prosperity. Between
January 1997 and December 1999, for example, 3.3 million employees –
who had been employed for three years or more – lost their jobs (Bureau of
Labor Statistics 2001).

From March 2001 the US was in recession. The effects of this were compounded by the September 11th attacks on New York and Washington DC.
Amidst uncertainty about both US and global trends, economic estimates and
projections were revised downwards.

Summary

The American dream – and its promise of upward economic mobility – is an
often cited phrase. However, although there is conflicting empirical evidence,
much of the data suggests that rates of mobility are limited, particularly for
women and minorities. Against this background, the unequal distribution of
income and wealth has considerable significance. Indeed, many now talk of an
underclass and overclass. While some hailed the new economy of the late
1990s as a revolutionary shift in the character of economic opportunity, the
claims were often exaggerated. Many features of the old economy remained.

References and further reading

Alsop, R. J. (ed.) (1998), *The Wall Street Journal Almanac 1999*, New York, Ballantine
    Books.
Bartlett, B. (2001), *The New Economy and Productivity Growth*, National Center for Policy
    Analysis, www.ncpa.org/oped/bartlett/bartlett01.html
Beck, R. (1996), *The Case Against Immigration: The Moral, Economic, Social and
    Environmental Reasons for Reducing US Immigration Back to Traditional Levels*, New
    York, W. W. Norton.
Bell, L. A. and R. B. Freeman (2000), *The Incentive for Working Hard: Explaining Hours
    Worked Differences in the US and Germany*, NBER Working Paper W8051, National
    Bureau of Economic Research, papers.nber.org/papers/W8051
Bellah, R. N., R. Madsen, W. M. Sullivan, A. Swidler and S. M. Tipton (1985), *Habits of
    the Heart: Individualism and Commitment in American Life*, Berkeley, University of
    California Press.
Bryner, G. (1998), *Politics and Public Morality: The Great American Welfare Reform Debate*,
    New York, W. W. Norton.
Bureau of Labor Statistics (2001), *Employment and Unemployment*, stats.bls.gov
Cohen, D. (2001), 'In search of a forgotten dream', *New Statesman*, 26 November, 32–5.
Cox, W. M. and R. Alm (1999), *Myths of Rich and Poor: Why We're Better Off Than We
    Think*, New York, BasicBooks.
Crevecoeur, J. H. S. J. (1986), *Letters from an American Farmer and Sketches of Eighteenth-
    Century America*, New York, Penguin.

Croly, H. (1989). *The Promise of American Life*, Boston, Northeastern University Press.

Drucker, P. (2001), 'The next society: a survey of the near future', *The Economist*, 3 November.

The Economist, 15 January 2000.

Featherman, D. L. and R. M. Hauser (1978), *Opportunity and Change*, New York, Academic Press.

Fletcher, M. A. (2000), 'Persistent poverty seen among Latinos in US', *International Herald Tribune*, 6 July, 3.

Furchtgott-Roth, D. and C. Stolba (1999), *Women's Figures: An Illustrated Guide to the Economic Progress of Women in America*, Washington DC/Arlington, The AEI Press/Independent Women's Forum.

General Social Survey (2001), *1972–2000 Cumulative Datafile*, csa.berkeley.edu: 7502/cgi-bin12/hsda3

Gilbert, D. and J. A. Kahl (1992), *The American Class Structure: A New Synthesis*, Belmont, Wadsworth Publishing.

Gittleman, M. and M. Joyce (1995), 'Earnings mobility in the United States, 1967–91', *Monthly Labor Review*, September, 3–13.

Greene J. P. (1993), *The Intellectual Construction of America*, Chapel Hill, University of North Carolina Press.

Hacker, A. (1995), *Two Nations: Black and White, Separate, Hostile, Unequal*, New York, Ballantine Books.

Hochschild, J. (1995), *Facing Up to the American Dream: Race, Class, and the Soul of the Nation*, Princeton, Princeton University Press.

Kingston, P. W. (2000), *The Classless Society*, Stanford, Stanford University Press.

Lasch, C. (1995), *The Revolt of the Elites and the Betrayal of Democracy*, New York, W. W. Norton.

Lind, M. (1996), *Up from Conservatism: Why the Right is Wrong for America*, New York, The Free Press.

Lipset S. M. and R. Bendix (1959), *Social Mobility in Industrial Society*, Berkeley and Los Angeles, University of California Press.

Lipset, S. M. (1997), *American Exceptionalism: A Double-Edged Sword*, New York, W. W. Norton.

Madrick, J. (2001), 'A tarnished new economy loses more luster with revised productivity data', *The New York Times*, 30 August.

Mahler, S. J. (1995), *American Dreaming: Immigrant Life on the Margins*, Princeton, Princeton University Press.

Massey D. S. and N. A. Denton (1993), *American Apartheid: Segregation and the Making of the Underclass*, Cambridge, MA, Harvard University Press.

McMurrer, D. P., M. Condon, and I. V. Sawhill (1997), *Intergenerational Mobility in the United States: A Companion Piece to The Declining Importance of Class*, Urban Institute, www.urban.org/oppor/opp_04b.htm

Murray, C. (1984), *Losing Ground: American Social Policy 1950–1980*, New York, BasicBooks.

National Center for Policy Analysis (2000a), *Economic Issues – Lag in Women's Pay Less Than Meets the Eye*, www.ncpa.org/pd/economy/pd051100c.html

National Center for Policy Analysis (2000b), *Bruce Bartlett Opinion Editorial: Income Inequality Rose Sharply Under Clinton*, 2 October, www.ncpa.org/oped/bartlett/oct0200.html

National Center for Policy Analysis (2001), *Idea House – Health Care Issues*, www.ncpa.org/health/pdh46.html

Nuechterlein, J. (2000), 'American dreaming', *First Things: A Monthly Journal of Religion and Public Life*, January, 11.

Pear, R. (2001), 'Number of uninsured drops for second year', *The New York Times*, 28 September.

Perry J. A. and E. K. Perry (2000), *Contemporary Society: An Introduction to Social Science*, Boston, Allyn & Bacon.

Rytina, S. (2000), 'Is occupational mobility declining in the US?' *Social Forces*, 78:4, June, 1227–76.

Sawhill, I. V. and D. P. McMurrer (1996a), *Economic Mobility in the United States: A Companion Piece to How Much do Americans Move Up and Down the Economic Ladder?*, Washington DC/New York, Urban Institute, www.urban.org/oppor/opp_031b.html

Sawhill, I. V. and D. P. McMurrer (1996b), *How Much do Americans Move Up and Down the Economic Ladder?*, Washington DC/New York, Urban Institute, www.urban.org/oppor/opp_031.htm

Sawhill, I. V. and D. P. McMurrer (1996c), 'American dreams and discontents: beyond the level playing field', *Opportunity in America*, 1, Washington DC, Urban Institute, www.urban.org/oppor/opp_01.htm

Seelye, K. Q. (2001), 'Poverty rates fell in 2000, but income was stagnant', *The New York Times*, 26 September.

Tuxeira, R. and J. Rogers (2000), *America's Forgotten Majority: Why the White Working Class Still Matters*, New York, BasicBooks.

Urban Institute (2001), 'Jobs and wages up sharply for single moms, gains especially high after welfare reform', *Single Parents' Earnings Monitor*, 25 July.

US Census Bureau (1999), *The Asian and Pacific Islander Population in the United States*, Washington DC, US Census Bureau.

US Census Bureau (2001a), *Historical Income Tables – Households, Table IE-1. Selected Measures of Household Income Dispersion: 1967 to 2000*, www.census.gov/hhes/income/histinc/ie1.html

US Census Bureau (2001b), *Historical Income Tables – People, Table P-2. Race and Hispanic Origin of People by Median Income and Sex: 1947 to 2000*, www.census.gov/hhes/income/histinc/p02.html

US Census Bureau (2001c), *Asset Ownership of Households*, www.census.gov/hhes/www/wealth/1995/wlth95-4.html

US Census Bureau (2001d), *Historical Income Tables – Households, Race and Hispanic Origin of Households by Median and Mean Income: 1967 to 2000*, www.census.gov/hhes/income/histinc/p02.html

US Census Bureau (2001e), *Statistical Abstract of the United States 2000*, US Census Bureau.

US Census Bureau (2001f), *Current Population Reports – Did You Know? Homes Account for 44 Percent of all Wealth*, Washington DC, US Department of Commerce.

Wright, J. W. (ed.) (2000), *The New York Times Almanac 2001*, New York, Penguin.

Wright, J. W. (ed.) (2001), *The New York Times Almanac 2002*, New York, Penguin.

3

Individualism and conformity

As Chapter 2 established, the American dream, and its promise of upward mobility, are rooted in economic individualism. There are, however, other forms of individualist thinking. Although it has always been partially restrained by notions of obligation towards family and community, American popular culture has traditionally emphasised the sovereignty of the individual. It has talked in terms of rights, liberties and the constraints that should be placed upon government. To an extent, it has also celebrated the willingness of particular individuals to defy convention, authority and the established order.

These sentiments are derived from two sources. First, there is an embedded belief in 'the . . . freedom to act as one desires, and the freedom to decide where one wants to live, to do as one likes, to believe what one wants, and so on' (quoted in van Elteren 1998: 44). This form of thinking – sometimes called expressive individualism – underpins the writings of Ralph Waldo Emerson (1803–82), the Transcendentalist essayist and poet. In calling for authentically American forms of culture and assertions of masculinity, Emerson wanted an all-pervading spirit of suspicious resentment: 'The nonchalance of boys who are sure of a good dinner, and would disdain as much as a lord to do or say aught to conciliate one, is the healthy attitude of human nature' (quoted in Allen 1970: 141).

The ideas associated with expressive individualism are also evident in the poetry of Walt Whitman (1819–92). In his collection, *Leaves of Grass*, Whitman tied together American identity, individualism and a sense of newness. He stressed the absolute freedom of choice open to the American citizen:

> Afoot and light-hearted I take to the open road,
> Healthy, free, the world before me,
> The long brown path before me, leading wherever I choose.
> (Quoted in Bellah *et al.* 1985: 34)

These themes were echoed a century later. During the 1950s the Beats – a group of writers and poets that included Jack Kerouac (1922–69), author of the 1957 book *On the Road*, and Allen Ginsberg – talked in terms of individual consciousness and the search for significant experience. Their work challenged the conformity and commercialism of the 1950s.

However, the place of the individual in popular iconography has a second source. It is drawn from particular representations of white male society in the South and West before the Civil War (1861–65). At that time, there were significant numbers of yeoman farmers. They lived in their own homesteads and were largely self-governing: 'They owned their own property, ruled their own families, ran their own farms and businesses, bore their own arms in their own defense, took responsibility for their own failures and mistakes . . . then and only then could men govern their own selves . . . as a republic' (Francis 1991: 9).

This vision of the American past led to an insistence that the property owner had an independence upon which others – including his neighbours – could not trample. Such thinking was tied to two closely associated strands of seventeenth-century thought. First, individuals originally had fundamental rights and liberties in the 'state of nature' that preceded the construction of ordered societies. Only some of these natural rights were relinquished when governments were formed. Others remained with the people – or at least those who were property-owning citizens – themselves. Furthermore, under the terms of the 'contract' established between governments and the governed, rights that had been delegated to the government could be reclaimed if it became repressive or failed to fulfil its obligations. There was therefore an emphasis upon liberty, due process of law and local self-rule, so that the powers assigned to government were always held in check.

Second, there is also a rudimentary labour theory of value. The land of individuals, and the other assets to which they laid claim, were theirs – and theirs alone – because they had, in almost every case, contributed their own labour and toil. As John Locke, the influential political philosopher argued, an individual would, through work and exertion, gain ownership and acquire rights: 'Whatsoever, then, he removes out of the state that Nature hath provided and left it in, he hath mixed his labour with it, and joined to it something that is his own, and thereby makes it his property' (quoted in Rifkin 2000: 79).

Economic and expressive individualism fuse together in another defining characteristic of American society. There is an impatience with permanence and stability. Instead, there have traditionally been relatively high levels of geographical mobility. Although the figures for 1999–2000 were relatively low compared with preceding years, 43.4 million American moved house (Schachter 2001). Statistics such as these have led one observer to talk in terms of a 'nomadic' culture: 'If students of the American character can agree upon any one thing, it is that compulsion to move about has created a nation of restless wanderers unlike any other in the world . . . When the fever strikes, the American goes, indifferent to the risks and scornful of that attachment to place that restrains the European' (quoted in Elazar 1994: 73).

Conformity and status insecurity

Seymour Martin Lipset (1961) suggests that conformist pressures are created by egalitarianism. American society is, as Chapter 1 noted, characterised by an 'equality of regard'. Although the US has always been profoundly unequal in terms of wealth and income, there was – in comparison with the countries of Europe – little deference and respect towards those from particular class backgrounds or those who occupied positions of authority. This leads to status uncertainty. It is always uncertain whether conspicuous spending, or achievement in sport, or victories on the battlefield will bring social recognition. Lipset has asserted that the British were – at least until the 1960s – secure in status terms because there was a recognised hierarchy in which each had an allotted place. As a consequence, they are relatively indifferent to criticism and are ready to speak out without fear of opprobrium. In contrast, because Americans are unsure and insecure about their social place, and see others as broadly their equals, they are reluctant to speak out or criticise others. Lipset and other observers have argued that conformity – and the reluctance to speak out that stems from egalitarian notions – is also evident in American attitudes towards children. The family is often child-oriented and it is widely said that children are spoilt by European standards. There is also, it is said, a lack of discipline in schools.

Conformity

Individualism still maintains a place in popular culture. The belief that individuals should be willing to confront and, where necessary, defy group sentiment has been a recurrent theme in literature, film and politics. It crosses traditional ideological cleavages. Sidney Lumet's 1957 film, *Twelve Angry Men*, represented a liberal celebration of one man's stand against mob instincts in the jury room. More conservative representations of individualism have drawn on notions of the self-reliant citizen and reiterated the right of individuals to defend themselves and their families and, where law enforcement agencies have failed to apprehend a suspect, to seek justice. In, for example, many Westerns and the *Dirty Harry* films, a lone individual acts outside the law where the authorities have, through indifference or cowardice, failed in their duties.

However, although popular culture still celebrates these themes, some observers have – from the earliest days of the US – lamented the loss of the individualist ethos. American identity seemed to be increasingly characterised by conformity and the citizen has been reluctant to dissent, stand alone or act differently. Even in the 1830s and 1840s, Alexis de Tocqueville warned that the 'empty phenomenon of public opinion is strong enough to chill innovators and to keep them silent and at a respectful distance' (quoted in Riesman 1962: 304). Another early European traveller, Harriet Martineau, who toured the US in 1830, similarly saw a 'fear of singularity'. There was, she argued, 'the restraint of perpetual caution, and reference to the opinions of others' (quoted in Lipset 1961: 143).

These fears assumed a starker and more comprehensive form in the years that followed the Second World War. In his 1950 book, *The Lonely Crowd*, David Riesman argued that the individualistic 'inner-directed' citizen was being displaced by those who were 'other-directed' and lacked personal autonomy. There had been, he asserted, 'a decline in individualism and a subversion of the desire to achieve' (quoted in Lipset 1961: 139). Riesman tied these changes to shifts in the character of technology. The modern industrial system had changed the nature of success and the means by which it could be achieved. In post-war America, success no longer depended upon individual effort, self-reliance and entrepreneurial initiative, but instead depended upon winning the good opinion of others and the courting of popularity (Lipset 1961: 139).

During the 1950s three processes seemed to confirm Riesman's fear that the US had become an increasingly passive and conformist society. First, there was a process of suburbanisation. The endless streets of mass-produced and prefabricated homes that were built to accommodate the exodus from the cities were described by Lewis Mumford in bitterly critical terms as 'a multitude of uniform, unidentifiable houses, lined up inflexibly, at uniform distances, on uniform roads, in a treeless communal wasteland, inhabited by people of the same class, the same income, the same age group' (quoted in Martin *et al.* 1993: 960). The Levittowns offered the most visible symbol of this. The first was built on Long Island by Levitt and Sons between 1947 and 1951. There were 17,447 low-cost homes and 75,000 residents. Further Levittowns were created in Pennsylvania and New Jersey. In contrast with earlier construction methods, the homes were mass produced and partially prefabricated using assembly line techniques. All were built to identical measurements and painted using the same green on ivory colour scheme (Ritzer 2000: 33–4). In the absence of distinctive features, the homes were marketed on the basis of their relative cheapness. Mass-produced housing, particularly when compounded by social homogeneity, led, it was said, to mass-produced lives.

Second, social roles were strictly defined. Women, in particular, seemed restricted to prescribed duties in the home. More and more women abandoned paid employment and become housewives as men began to obtain a real wage that was sufficient to support an entire family. Women defined themselves in terms of their role as wives and mothers. Betty Friedan, whose 1963 book *The Feminine Mystique* contributed to the emergence and growth of the feminist movement, remembered life in the suburban home and the basis of its appeal:

> At home, you were necessary, you were important, you were the boss, in fact – the mother . . . I was more than ready to embrace the feminine mystique. I took a

cooking course and started studying the suburban real-estate ads. And the next time the census taker came around . . . I said self-consciously, virtuously, with only the faintest stirrings of protest from that part of me I'd turned my back on – 'housewife'. (Quoted in Henretta, Brownlee, Brody and Ware 1993: 910)

Many of the television series produced during the period celebrated the nuclear family and the different roles assigned to man and wife. *I Love Lucy*, for example, warned of the pitfalls awaiting women who sought a career or circumvented their husband's wishes (Coontz 1997: 38). Psychological studies buttressed popular culture by stressing the importance of the mother–child relationship. If, it was argued, children were deprived of motherly love and attention, they could become delinquent or psychopathic. A mother's place was at home with her children.

Alongside suburbanisation and a seemingly narrow definition of social roles, the growth of **mass culture** also appeared to confirm Riesman's pessimism. Individuals, it was said, were being turned into passive recipients of a mass culture structured around soap operas, quiz shows and standardised self-help guides that eliminated the creativity and imagination associated with particular tasks. People were increasingly vulnerable to manipulation by organised interests and hidden social forces. In *The Hidden Persuaders*, Vance Packard warned that the advertising industry was manufacturing wants and needs among the American people. He noted 'the growing conformity and sterility of their life where they are left only with the roles of being consumers or spectators' (quoted in Kammen 1999: 196).

Little boxes

The growth of the American suburbs – and the building of almost identical mass produced homes – was gently mocked by Pete Seeger in a popular song:

Little boxes on the hillside,
Little boxes made of ticky tacky
Little boxes on the hillside,
Little boxes all the same.

Qualifying conformity

However, these representations of America as a society in which individuals are subordinated to an all-encompassing commercialism need to be qualified. First, the degree to which there was social conformity should not be exaggerated. Although American society appears tightly bound during the 1950s and early 1960s, there were strains just below the surface.

For example, despite apparent family stability, there were suggestions that many relationships had an unhappy and destructive character. Edward Albee's play, *Who's Afraid of Virginia Wolf?*, first performed in 1962, depicted a middle-aged couple living on a New England college campus. Their bickering quickly gives way to uncontrolled rage. *The Graduate*, a 1967 film directed by Mike Nichols, similarly represented suburban life in terms of boredom and superficiality. Many couples appear to have stayed together in largely empty relationships. They were bound to each other by the stigma, as well as the legal and financial difficulties, attached to separation and divorce. Furthermore, despite the sense of conformity and moral propriety that appeared to define the character of the era, the Kinsey reports on sexual behaviour indicated that many Americans had rather less conventional private lives. Although doubts were subsequently raised about the reports' accuracy and methodology, they suggested that about half of husbands had extra-marital sex during their lives and that 37 per cent of all men had some homosexual experience (Kinsey, Pomeroy and Martin 1948: 585, 623).

The racial order in the southern states was also beginning – under the weight of protests – to be dismantled. In 1954 the US Supreme Court ruled, in *Brown* v. *Board of Education* (Topeka, Kansas), that segregated public education – relegating black children to separate and unequal schools – was unconstitutional. In 1956 federal troops took control in Little Rock, Arkansas, as black students began to take their places in integrated classrooms. The 1955 boycott in Montgomery, Alabama, led to desegregation on the city's buses. At the end of the decade, although there had still been few legislative reforms, the civil rights movement had established itself.

There were other undercurrents in the 1950s. The role of the Beat generation has already been noted. The music of the era also suggests that conformity was largely confined to surface appearance. Rock and roll artists such as Elvis Presley challenged traditional sexual mores and appropriated musical forms – most notably the blues – that had been hitherto associated with African-Americans. At the same time, *Mad* magazine knew few taboos and some of the best-known films of the period – such as *The Wild One* (1951) and *Rebel Without a Cause* (1955) – also stressed rebellion.

During the decade that followed, dissidence took a more overt form. In June 1962 radical students – organised by Students for a Democratic Society (SDS) – issued the Port Huron statement. It offered, in its own words, an 'agenda for a generation . . . bred in at least modest comfort, housed now in universities, looking uncomfortably at the world we inherit'. It called participatory democracy 'rooted in love, reflectiveness, reason and creativity' (quoted in Morton Blum 1992: 99). At the same time, some forms of popular music, most notably Bob Dylan's early songs, built upon the implicitly subversive character of rock and roll by adopting an explicit message of revolt. In *With God on Our Side*, Dylan scorned Cold War ideologies. He placed himself alongside the civil rights movement in *Only a Pawn in Their Game* and expressed a more generalised message of social and political dissent in *The Times They Are A-Changin'*.

As the decade progressed, and as the Vietnam War escalated, social criticism widened its horizons. 'Alternative' lifestyles – such as those associated with flower power, hippies, yippies and the Woodstock generation – took root in some of the larger cities. At the same time, the nuclear family structure, within which women abandoned paid employment and worked solely as wives and mothers, was eroded by economic shifts and challenged by those who saw it as oppressive. As the long economic boom came towards a close, and family aspirations grew in response to an expanding range of consumer durables, large numbers of women – including the mothers of young children – sought full or part-time employment outside of the home. Radical psychiatry suggested that the relationships engendered by the nuclear family were inherently dysfunctional. Feminism put forward a critique of both the family and traditional gender roles. Both, it was said, reflected patriarchal interests. They subordinated the interests of women to the needs of men. Although radical feminism was confined to the political margins, the assumptions of the earlier era – and representations of women in conventionally feminine terms – were ridiculed in films such as *The Stepford Wives*.

The radical critique

Notions of mass culture, and claims that the US has a regimented and conformist character, have not been confined to the 1950s. They contributed to the critique of American society put forward by the New Left during the upheavals of the late 1960s and early 1970s. Harry Braverman, a Marxist critic and author of *Labor and Monopoly Capitalism*, which was first published in 1974, stresses the effects of changes in the industrial process. He sees the adoption of Taylorism by American companies as critical. In his 1911 book, Frederick W. Taylor called for the adoption of scientific management. Industrial efficiency, he argued, demanded the introduction of time and motion studies. Each part of the production cycle was to be broken down into its components and subjected to 'rules, laws and formulae'. Workers should not have to plan or think about their actions. Instead, the labour process should rest on routine and the simplification of tasks. Taylor's methods and a system of payment by results – or piece rates – were widely adopted by companies such as Ford in Detroit. They led – particularly when tied to the introduction of the conveyor-belt and assembly line – to dramatic increases in both production and productivity levels. However, as Braverman argues, scientific management reduced workers to the status of mere commodities. All their actions were subject to management *diktat*.

Braverman's analysis has its roots in classical Marxism. Others associated with radical politics turned to the Frankfurt school and critical theory. There was talk of the **authoritarian personality**. According to Theodor Adorno, some people – particularly those raised by strict fathers or who were accorded little affection as young children – attached great importance to traditional values and had uncritically conformist attitudes. They deferred to those in authority, but were at the same time hostile towards minorities or those who defied the prevailing cultural rules. The work of others associated with the Frankfurt school also attracted attention. Herbert Marcuse (1898–1979), a German émigré who continued his work as a philospher in the US after the Nazis took power, argued in books such as *One Dimensional Man* (1964) that – in advanced industrial economies – individuals are subject to manipulation and control. They have been integrated into the economic, political and cultural system and effective opposition has been eliminated. The working class that Marx and his followers saw as the harbinger of revolution had, Marcuse asserted, been incorporated. This process stifled criticism, protest and dissent. Higher living standards, consumer durables, the creation of 'false needs' through modern advertising, and restricting the genuine freedom of the individual had reduced individual hopes and aspirations to the acquisition of further consumer goods. Indeed, consumerism also fulfilled spiritual wants: 'The people recognize themselves in their commodities; they find their soul in their automobile, hi-fi set, split-level home, kitchen equipment' (quoted in Haralambos and Holborn 2000: 690).

Although thoughts of revolution and many of the concepts associated with Marxism lost much of their former credence, some radical critiques of American society continued to attract attention during the 1980s and 1990s. Neil Postman, a communications theorist, describes the US as a **technopoly**. Contemporary society is, he argues, governed by – and subordinate to – technology. This was largely because – as the twentieth century progressed – technological developments addressed almost every human need:

> To every Old World belief, habit, or tradition, there was and still is a technological alternative. To prayer, the alternative is penicillin; to family roots, the alternative is mobility; to reading, the alternative is television; to restraint, the alternative is immediate gratification; to sin, the alternative is psychotherapy . . . There is even an alternative to the painful riddle of death . . . The riddle may be postponed through longer life, and then perhaps solved altogether by cryogenics. (Postman 1993: 54)

George Ritzer talks of 'McDonaldization'. Echoing Braverman's critique of scientific management, he sees McDonald's – the fast food chain established by Ray Kroc in 1955 – as the harbinger of a far-reaching economic and cultural shift. McDonaldization rests upon a process of standardisation that affects both the consumer and the worker. Consumers have only a limited degree of choice between products that always take an identical form. Furthermore, their behaviour in the restaurant is regulated: the physical environment is deliberately designed to ensure that customers do not linger once the food has been eaten. For their part, the workers are tied to assembly-line forms of production and distribution. Their working day is continually controlled and monitored. 'Fast-food restaurants try in many ways to make workers look, act, and think more predictably . . . Training programs are designed to indoctrinate the worker into a "corporate culture" . . . Incentives (awards, for example) are used to reward employees who behave properly, and disincentives, ultimately firing, to deal with those who do not' (Ritzer 2000: 92).

Benjamin Barber has emphasised the way in which the process of McDonaldization has permeated much of the world. In particular, it has shaped and structured much of industry, commerce, cultural production and the new information sector. Although challenged by assertions of identity – such as those expressed in militant Islam – the process of globalisation has hastened the growth of 'McWorld' and the increasing irrelevance of the traditional nation-state and established frontiers. The ubiquitous character of MTV and McDonald's itself are visible expressions of this. Furthermore, McWorld is increasingly absorbing activities that were traditionally the non-commercial building blocks of civil society: 'Coke has successfully purchased the once civic-minded song "We Are the World" . . . and Disney is founding "schools" and study "institutes" in Florida while building whole new towns like "Celebration" to promote its multiplying wares . . . Bill Gates, CEO of Microsoft, has begun to buy up the world of culture' (Barber 1996: 294).

However, although critiques such as these have attracted considerable attention, they sometimes have – like *The Lonely Crowd* decades earlier – a one-dimensional character. Although the adoption of scientific management bolstered management control and – according to its critics – robbed workers of their identity, it also provoked resistance and opposition. Mass production – and the homogenisation of labour – led many to join labour unions. In the contemporary US, large corporations and standardisation have been displaced by the growth of small-scale niche markets and more assertive forms of consumerism.

Summary

American individualism traditionally incorporated notions of freedom and a willingness to confront established order. However, although these themes still find a place in popular culture, there have been recurrent fears that individualism is being suppressed by modernisation. The process of suburbanisation in the 1950s and early 1960s seemed to usher in a conformist society. However, there were always dissident undercurrents and these assumed a more explicit form in the 1960s. Since then, Marxist and post-Marxist critiques of American society have stressed the subordination of the individual to the labour process, the regulation of everyday life, and 'McDonaldization'.

References and further reading

Allen, W. (1970), *The Urgent West: An Introduction to the Idea of the United States*, London, Readers Union.

Alsop, R. J. (ed.) (1998), *The Wall Street Journal Almanac 1999*, New York, Ballantine Books.

Barber, B. R. (1996), *Jihad vs. McWorld: How Globalism and Tribalism are Reshaping the World*, New York, Ballantine Books.

Bellah, R. N., R. Madsen, W. M. Sullivan, A. Swidler and S. M. Tipton (1985), *Habits of the Heart: Individualism and Commitment in American Life*, Berkeley, University of California Press.

Braverman, H. and J. B. Foster (1999), *Labor and Monopoly Capitalism*, New York, Monthly Review Press.

Bureau of Justice Statistics (2001), *Nation's Violent Crime Rate Fell almost 15 Percent Last Year – Property Crime Down 10 Percent*, www.ojp.usdoj.gov/bjs/pub/press/cv00pr.htm

Coontz, S. (1997), *The Way We Really Are: Coming to Terms with America's Changing Families*, New York, BasicBooks.

Derber, C. (1996), *The Wilding of America: How Greed and Violence are Eroding our Nation's Character*, New York, St Martin's Press.

Elazar, D. J. (1994), *The American Mosaic: The Impact of Space, Time, and Culture on American Politics*, Boulder, Westview Press.

Francis, S. T. (1991), 'Principalities and Powers', *Chronicles*, August, 8–10.

Glendon, M. A. (1991), *Rights Talk: The Impoverishment of Political Discourse*, New York, The Free Press.

Haralambos, M. and M. Holborn (2000), *Sociology: Themes and Perspectives*, London, Collins.

Henretta, J. A., W. E. Brownlee, D. Brody and S. Ware (1993), *America's History*, New York, Worth Publishers.

Kammen, M. (1999), *American Culture and Tastes: Social Change and the Twentieth Century*, New York, BasicBooks.

Kinsey, A. C., W. B. Pomeroy and C. E. Martin (1948), *Sexual Behavior in the Human Male*, Philadelphia, W. B. Saunders Co.

Lasch, C. (1980), *The Culture of Narcissism: American Life in an Age of Diminishing Expectations*, New York, Warner Books.

Lipset, S. M. (1961), 'A changing American character?', in S. M. Lipset and L. Lowenthal (eds), *Culture and Social Character: The Work of David Riesman Reviewed*, New York, The Free Press of Glencoe, 136–71.

Marcuse, H. (1964), *One Dimensional Man: Studies in the Ideology of Advanced Industrial Society*, Boston, Beacon Press.

Martin, J. K., R. Roberts, S. Mintz, L. O. McMurry and J. H. Jones (1993), *America and its People*, New York, HarperCollins.

Morton Blum, J. (1992), *Years of Discord: American Politics and Society, 1961–1974*, New York, W. W. Norton.

Murray, C. (1984), *Losing Ground: American Social Policy 1950–1980*, New York, BasicBooks.

Postman, N. (1993), *Technopoly: The Surrender of Culture to Technology*, New York, Vintage Books.

Riesman, D. (1962), *The Lonely Crowd: A Study of the Changing American Character*, New Haven, Yale University Press.

Rifkin, J. (2000), *The Age of Access: The New Culture of Hypercapitalism, Where All of Life is a Paid-For Experience*, New York, Jeremy P. Tarcher.

Ritzer, G. (2000), *The McDonaldization of Society*, Thousand Oaks, Pine Forge Press.

Schachter, J. (2001), *Current Population Reports – Geographical Mobility, March 1999 to March 2000*, US Census Bureau, www.census.gov/prod/2001pubs/p20-538.pdf

Van Elteren, M. (1998), 'The Riddles of Individualism and Community in American and Dutch Society', *Journal of American Culture*, 21:1, 43–80.

4

Communities, civic decline and 'bowling alone'

Studies of American identity have traditionally emphasised the role of individualism, the different forms that it takes and the part it has played in shaping the contours of American society. However, although individualism is at the core of American identity, it has, in practice, never been unchecked or unfettered. While the US has long celebrated the lone individual and the pursuit of self-interest, American identity has at the same time reined in the individualist ethos. Alongside individualism, it also stresses the importance of the ties that bind individuals to families, kinship networks, communities, civic organisations, particular localities, ethnic groupings and the American nation itself.

Early Puritanism – which contributed to the moulding of both New England and the governing American ideology or 'creed' – reflected this. It drew upon theological individualism and, in contrast with Roman Catholicism or 'high' Anglicanism, which placed the priest as an intermediary – or intercessor – between the individual and God, emphasised the direct accountability of the sinner to the Almighty. As Loren Baritz records, Puritan theology stressed: 'individualism – one sinner before God, no institutional or priestly intercessors, no Virgin Mary, to smooth things over . . . They believed that salvation lay in each individual's heart and soul' (Baritz 1990: 4).

However, the early Puritan settlements also bequeathed a communal tradition. John Winthrop (1588–1649), who organised the migration of thousands of settlers from England and served as the first governor of the Massachusetts Bay Colony, emphasised the importance of mutual ties in a sermon that he gave just before the settlers landed: 'We must delight in each other, make others conditions our own, rejoyce together, mourn together, labor and suffer together, always having before our eyes our community as members of the same body' (quoted in Bellah *et al.* 1985: 28).

The New England towns that emerged from these beginnings were shaped by these origins. They had an organic character. There were few extensive contacts with the outside world and the inhabitants were tied to each other by religious consensus. While there was some commerce and trade, the market was

---

Individualism and social solidarity

The relationship between individualism and the 'pull' associated with family, community and nation has been depicted in different ways. Most suggest that there is a tension between them. However, there are differences about their relative weight. Daniel Bell suggests that the informal and formal networks that form the basis of civil society are the defining characteristic of American society (Bell 1991: 60). In contrast, Claude S. Fischer asserts that communal instincts have always been subordinate to individual self-interest and personal advancement. In a study of attitudes towards local communities, he concludes that although most Americans value the fellowship offered in communities – insofar as they provide a degree of security in a largely atomised society – there are limits to communalism. 'They often resist that same local community . . . when it constrains their interests, be the constraints in taxes, behavioral codes, or infringements of private property . . . While Americans value the locality as solidarity, it takes second place to individual freedom' (quoted in van Elteren 1998: 52).

Others, however, question the assertion that there is a tension between individualism and social solidarity. Individual self-interest, they suggest, leads to the creation of ties and co-operation. Although this form of argument is, today, associated with some within the conservative Right, it underpinned many of Alexis de Tocqueville's commentaries on early American life. As he asserted: 'An enlightened regard for themselves constantly prompts them to assist each other, and inclines them willingly to sacrifice a portion of their time and property to the welfare of the State' (Tocqueville 1965: 393). Furthermore, 'they are free, but exposed to a thousand accidents; and experience soon teaches them that, although they do not habitually require the assistance of others, a time almost certainly comes when they cannot do without it' (Tocqueville 1965: 443).

---

constrained by relationships based upon mutual obligation. Although communities were looser in the other regions of colonial America, particularly the South, they were still structured around particular localities, close personal networks and shared customs. The small town continued to subordinate market forces – and the efforts of individuals to better themselves – to a sense of collective belonging until long into the nineteenth century: 'The competitive individualism stirred by commerce was balanced and humanized by the restraining influences of a fundamentally egalitarian ethic of community responsibility' (Bellah *et al.* 1985: 38).

Associations and organisations

The collective networks, voluntary associations and organisations that formed a counterweight to individualism were the building blocks of **civil society**.

Alexis de Tocqueville's reports emphasised their role as a defining characteristic of American life:

> Americans of all ages, all conditions, and all dispositions, constantly form associations. They have not only commercial and manufacturing companies, in which all take part, but associations of a thousand other kinds – religious, moral, serious, futile, extensive or restricted, enormous or diminutive. The Americans make associations to give entertainments, to found establishments for education, to build inns, to construct churches, to diffuse books, to send missionaries to the antipodes; and in this manner they found hospitals, prisons, and schools. (Tocqueville 1965: 376)

Some observers have suggested that these ties and connections were largely destroyed during the late nineteenth and early twentieth centuries by commercialism and the process of urbanisation. Increasing numbers lived in cities rather than the small town. Local businesses, small companies and family firms – which had personal ties with many of those they served on a daily basis – were absorbed or displaced by the large corporation. In comparison with the past, such corporations seemed faceless and anonymous. They appeared interested only in the accumulation of profit. At the same time, local voluntary organisations and societies were absorbed into national structures and organisations. Their headquarters were often far removed from the individual branch or chapter.

Those who emphasise developments such as these often employ the distinction drawn by Ferdinand Tonnies, an early sociologist. He represented traditional communities in terms of *Gemeinschaft*, based upon group solidarity and close, long-established relationships. In contrast to this, he argued, urban and metropolitan life was structured around *Gesellschaft*, an 'artificial construction of an aggregate of human beings' (quoted in Bender 1993: 17). Whereas the small town offered a structured sense of belonging and place, cities such as New York, Chicago and Los Angeles appeared to be characterised by isolation, instrumentalism – insofar as relationships existed only to serve particular purposes – and a sense of *anomie*.

However, all of this may be too stark. There is evidence to suggest that elements of *Gemeinschaft* continued to co-exist alongside the *Gesellschaft* of urban society. Thomas Bender argues that social change was an uneven and differentiated process. Indeed, in some instances urbanisation strengthened rather than weakened the basic ties of community. Many of the ethnic neighbourhoods that took shape in the bigger cities, organised around particular immigrant groupings, were structured by kinship networks and communal institutions. There were networks of voluntary groupings and organisations. In the midst of a mass society, identity was, in part, nurtured by these ties. As Bender notes: 'Small circles of "we" characterised by sameness and even parochialism nourish and secure part of everyone's identities, but everyone is also engaged in a broader and more public sense of the "we"' (Bender 1998: 140).

During the first half of the twentieth century, the numbers enrolled in voluntary and fraternal organisations that provided mutual assistance – such as the Elks, the Scouts, and Women's Clubs – grew steadily, although their growth was checked during the depression of the 1930s. There was a particularly intense period of growth during the two decades that followed the Second World War. Robert Putnam has recorded the rise of parent–teacher associations (PTAs): 'On average, every year throughout the quarter century up to 1960 another 1.6 percent of all American families with kids – more than 400,000 families a year – was added to the PTA membership rolls. Year after year, more and more parents became involved in this way in their children's education' (Putnam 2000: 56).

This was the era of the 'long, civic generation' comprising those born between 1910 and 1940 (Putnam 2000: 254). For many, the Second World War was a formative experience. It was a period of intense patriotism and

---

The immigrant communities

Both Robert Putnam and his critics talk in broad – perhaps sweeping – terms. There are, however, important differences between the character of life in the cities, suburbs and rural regions. In particular, the immigrant communities – many of which are located in the cities – demand attention.

Some observers are associated with the ethnic solidarity school. They emphasise the degree of reciprocity and co-operation in the immigrant enclaves. Many immigrants, for example, depend upon systems of rotating credit that enable them to establish entrepreneurial ventures and pay the initial capital back at a later stage. Others, however, suggest that, in low income communities, mutual co-operation is threatened by the need for money. Individuals have to seek additional income from within their own communities through both formal and informal enterprise.

> When immigrants discover, for instance, that they have to pay rent in the United States, an expense they may never have faced in their homelands, they devise ways to sublet housing to minimize their payments; in some cases, they actually make money off the rental. When they discover that private cars are essential to transportation on Long Island, they offset the maintenance costs by using these vehicles as informal taxis for fellow immigrants. (Mahler 1995: 217)

Sara Mahler suggests that the commercialisation of relationships within the communities – and the search for revenue from other immigrants – undermines mutual trust and co-operation.

there was a strong sense of civic duty. Many men and some women had served in the armed forces and those who were too young were enrolled in organisations such as the Junior Service Corps or the Junior Red Cross. Although there were severe racial tensions in some cities, there was also a sense of social solidarity.

Such attitudes bred a sense of civic duty that appears to have lasted long after the war had come to a close. Furthermore, the belief that individuals had responsibilities and duties was more ingrained in the US than in Western Europe. As Gabriel Almond and Sidney Verba found in their 1963 study, *The Civic Culture*, the active citizen – who is committed to civic affairs – was held in high regard. Some 51 per cent of Americans believed that the ordinary person should be a participant in community affairs. In contrast, the figures for the UK and Germany were 39 per cent and 22 per cent respectively (Almond and Verba 1989: 127).

Bowling alone

In January 1995 Robert D. Putnam's essay, 'Bowling alone', was published in the *Journal of Democracy*. Although working at Harvard University, Putnam was little known outside the world of political science, and the *Journal of Democracy* had only a small, largely academic readership. Furthermore, some of Putnam's concerns had been raised in earlier years by communitarian theorists, most notably Robert Bellah and his co-authors in their 1985 study, *Habits of the Heart*. Nonetheless, 'Bowling alone' generated a debate that engaged intellectuals, columnists, think-tanks and sections of the American public. Indeed, Putnam himself met with President Clinton and his thinking found expression in the State of the Union address.

Putnam's essay – later expanded and published in book form – was a study of group membership, civic engagement and 'social connectedness'. Putnam argues that despite higher levels of education – which are usually tied to increasing civic engagement – participation rates in voluntary organisations had fallen during the closing decades of the twentieth century. He notes, for example, that involvement in parent–teacher associations dropped from more than 12 million to barely 5 million in 1982. The labour unions, churches and fraternal organisations had all been subject to a similar process of decline. Nor was the process confined to organised and structured groupings. Ties had loosened within the family as single parenthood and stepfamilies became more common. Putnam cites surveys suggesting that the proportion of Americans who socialise has dropped significantly. In the mid to late-1970s the average American entertained friends on fourteen or fifteen occasions a year. By the late 1990s the figure had fallen to eight (Putnam 2000: 98). Other activities traditionally undertaken with friends – such as card playing – also dropped to a significant extent.

Putnam suggests that, at the same time, plain and simple neighbourliness had also tailed off. For example, the frequency with which individuals 'spend a social evening with someone who lives in your neighborhood' fell by about a third between 1974 and 1998 (Putnam 2000: 105). Sports and recreation were similarly affected, and this provided the basis for the title of Putnam's essay. Activities that were once pursued on a team basis have become individual pursuits. Although the total number of bowlers increased by 10 per cent between 1980 and 1993, the numbers participating in league bowling fell by 40 per cent during the same period. Americans, Putnam asserts, are now quite literally 'bowling alone'.

Putnam acknowledges that some new groups and organisations had emerged to take the place of those that had lost members. In the 1970s and 1980s women's organisations and environmental groups had, in particular, made a mark. The American Association of Retired Persons (AARP) grew from just 400,000 in 1960 to 33 million in 1993 (Putnam 1995). However, although advocacy organisations such as the AARP are well represented in Washington DC, they are not based upon the active involvement and participation of their members:

> Though these new groups often depend on financial support from ordinary citizens and may speak faithfully on their behalf, they are not really composed of citizen members in the same sense that a church congregation or a reading group or a fraternal organization is . . . The AARP is politically significant, but it demands little of its members' energies and contributes little to their social capital . . . In many respects, such organizations have more in common with mail-order commercial organizations than with old-fashioned face-to-face associations. (Putnam 2000: 51)

Putnam is not a lone voice. Others have also argued that American society is becoming increasingly fragmented. Some point to the growth of **edge cities** based around the sprawling metropolitan and suburban regions that have grown up around once discrete cities. In contrast with traditional neighbourhoods and communities, there is little spatial concentration. Instead, although much of the most sought-after housing is in the vicinity of the better schools,cities have multiple centres. Employment, residence and urban services – such as schools and retail stores – are all in different locations. At the same time, because of changes in the character of the economy, the nature of employment has changed. Increasingly, it is relatively short term and individuals shift between jobs.

Against this background, relationships often have an instrumental character. Networks of friends and associates are formed on the basis of the assistance that they can offer in gaining new employment or a place at a particular school: 'individuals' networks shift from neighbors and fellow community members to contacts in "destinational" institutions such as work and schools' (Carnoy 2000: 162). These networks are therefore short term and, some would suggest, superficial in character. As Carnoy puts it: 'If you don't like the ties that bind you to others – for even the most ephemeral or transitory or stupid reasons – you can and may leave' (Garreau quoted in Carnoy 2000: 163)

Crime

The number of violent crimes reported to the authorities rose from 288,460 in 1960 to 1,820,130 in 1990. Different explanations for this were put forward. Charles Derber (1996) suggested that it could be attributed, at least in part, to 'wilding', a perverted expression of individualism. For their part, conservative commentators pointed to public policy changes and cultural shifts. Charles Murray argued that both the chances of arrest – and the likelihood of a punishment being imposed – dropped significantly during this period. This altered the balance between disincentives and incentives and encouraged some to engage in criminal forms of behaviour (Murray 1984: 170). Murray also points to the growth of illegitimacy that he attributes, in turn, to the system of welfare provision that preceded the passage of the 1996 Personal Responsibility and Work Opportunity Act. Financial assistance had enabled young women to have babies outside of a family relationship. Children therefore grew up without a father figure and instead looked for other role models, such as those provided in street gangs. Furthermore, young men were not 'tamed' by the responsibilities associated with family life. All of this, Murray asserts, constituted a seedbed for criminality.

However, despite the fears expressed by conservatives, the crime rate leveled off and began to fall during the 1990s. By 1999, the number of violent crimes had dropped to 1,430,690. There was a decline of 28.3 per cent in the violent crime rate per 100,000 inhabitants between 1990 and 1999 (Wright 2001: 307). Why did this happen? The economic boom offered increased employment opportunities and the decline in poverty levels ameliorated some hardship. The long-term fall in the birth rate also played a part. There were, proportionately, fewer young men, the grouping most prone to commit criminal acts. Mandatory prison sentences and the 'zero tolerance' policing methods pursued by, for example, former New York Mayor Rudolph Giuliani, may also have contributed to the reduction in the crime figures. Sometimes known as the 'broken windows' policy, they owed much to James Q. Wilson from the University of California at Los Angeles. He emphasised the way in which graffiti, neglect, small-scale acts of anti-social behaviour, and broken windows created an atmosphere in a particular neighbourhood that encouraged violent crime to take root. If the police addressed these low-level problems, he argued, there would also be a decline in more serious forms of criminality.

The politics of disengagement

If Putnam's critique is accepted, there are important social, political and economic consequences. Francis Fukuyama, author of the controversial study *The End of History and the Last Man*, suggests that civic engagement and civil society, and the mutual trust around which they were constructed, have long served as a counterweight to the individualism of American culture (Fukuyama 1996: 272). The decline of solidarity and trust has led to a more unfettered assertion of individualism. Indeed, Robert Bellah and the co-authors of *Habits of the Heart*, a communitarian critique first published in 1985, spoke of **hyperindividualism**. Whereas traditional individualism was always constrained by a sense of obligation to others and the American dream, which was structured around self-discipline, hyperindividualism rests upon immediate self-gratification and self-expression, regardless of the consequences for others. Increasingly, it is argued, the individual is sovereign and unbound. The hyperindividualist ethos is eroding collective structures and the building blocks of civil society.

Mary Ann Glendon suggests that the character of legal discourse has changed and there is an increasingly rights-based culture. In contrast with the countries of Europe, rights – which are assigned to the lone individual rather than to institutions or collective associations – are not associated with corresponding duties and responsibilities. Instead, she asserts, they are represented as entitlements. Disputes therefore take an absolutist form: 'The language of rights is the language of no compromise. The winner takes all and the loser has to get out of town. The conversation is over' (Glendon 1991: 9).

Other commentators go further and assert that hyperindividualism has created a sense of isolation and fear. Francis Fukuyama cites the 1992 killing of a Japanese student in Louisiana who had mistakenly knocked on a front door. The owner took fright: 'The home owner, holed up in his private fortress and so distrustful of the outside world that he was ready to shoot a neighborhood teenager who came to his front door, is the very image of social isolation' (Fukuyama 1996: 310).

Writing from a liberal perspective, Charles Derber argues that the absolutist disregard of others has given rise to a 'wilding' culture. It is, he asserts, 'a degenerate form of individualism' (Derber 1996: 9). Defined strictly, a 'wilding' is New York street slang for an attack on an innocent victim. The word entered the vocabulary in April 1989 when a jogger was gang-raped by a group of teenagers in Central Park (Derber 1996: 1–2). Derber applies the term to a broad range of illegal and legal activities. He includes, for example, the killing of other family members by individuals such as Susan Smith, the South Carolina mother who killed her own young children, and the Menendez brothers who murdered their parents so as to inherit their estate and gain an insurance payment. However, he also points to what he regards as the ruthless pursuit of profit and talks of 'corporate wilding' and, in particular, cites those who made millions from 'junk bonds' and through the exploitation of cheap labour. The growth of wilding is rooted in both hyperindividualism and economic circumstances. It is, Derber asserts, 'a corruption of the American dream . . . the traditional restraints on naked self-aggrandisement seem weaker – and the insatiability greater . . . But when real income begins to decline . . . an outsized Dream becomes illusion . . . To weave materialist dreams in an era of restricted opportunities is the ultimate recipe for social wilding' (Derber 1996: 13).

For some associated with liberalism, civil society traditionally played an important role in constraining both the apparatus of government and commercial interests. It is, according to Benjamin Barber from Rutgers University, a societal dwelling place that is neither a capitol building nor a shopping mall it 'occupies the middle ground between government and the private sector' (Barber 1996:281). If, however, the structures of civil society begin to crumble, both the state and the market begin to fill the vacuum that has been created. Day-to-day life is, as a consequence, subject to further **commercialisation** and increasing state direction.

For his part, Robert Putnam has argued that the process of disengagement and the loss of trust have had consequences for the 'quality of governance'. There has been growing detachment from the political process. The proportion of the voting age population that casts a ballot in US presidential elections has fallen from 63.06 per cent in 1960 to 49.08 per cent in 1996. Other forms of political participation have also tailed off. Attendance at political meetings has dropped and there has been a marked decline in the numbers willing to work for a party. There has been a corresponding rise in the proportion of the population that has lost its faith in political institutions. Those unwilling to 'trust' the federal government rose from about 30 per cent in 1966 to 75 per cent in 1992. Furthermore, Putnam argues, good government depended upon the extent to which there are social bonds and ties among those living in a particular region. This is partly because civil associations teach and inculcate the procedures and customs upon which a democratic society rests. As he told an interviewer: 'You learn the personal virtues and skills that are the prerequisites for a democracy. Listening, for example. Taking notes. Keeping minutes. Taking responsibility for your views. That's what is different about league bowling versus bowling alone' (American Association for Higher Education 1995).

Civic disengagement and declining levels of trust also have economic implications. Formal and informal associations constitute 'social capital'. Like physical capital (machinery and equipment), it serves as a basis for economic development and increasing the organisational efficiency of companies. Trust in others, social networks, co-operation and the pooling of resources reduce the time and money – described by economists as **transaction costs** – that must otherwise be devoted to finding information, ensuring that guidelines and instructions are being met, and ascertaining the integrity of others.

Hyperindividualism and the pursuit of unfettered self-interest have, some suggest, corrupted the character of popular culture. The late Christopher Lasch, an influential social theorist who contributed much towards communitarian thinking, pointed to shifts in the use of language: 'It is symptomatic of the underlying tenor of American life that vulgar terms for sexual intercourse also convey the sense of getting the better of someone, working him over, taking him in, imposing your will through guile, deception, or superior force' (Lasch 1980: 66). Lasch added a further point. Individualism has also given way among some to narcissism. People have retreated towards impulsive self-obsession. They seek therapeutic solutions to their troubles based upon 'the feeling, the momentary illusion, of personal well-being, health and psychic security' (Lasch 1980: 7). They have no set goals or aspirations. Instead: 'Wants themselves become formless and unspecifiable. To the question, "what do they want, then?" there is only one answer in the case of people whose desires are unformed by the experience of participating in a culture larger than themselves: "Everything"' (quoted in Glendon 1991: 173).

Religion

Although the First Amendment to the Constitution established that there should be no established church – which in the 1960s led the US Supreme Court to end prayer and other forms of worship in public schools – religious faith has deep roots in the US. A 1993 study suggested that attendance is more than three times higher in the US than in Britain (Gallup and Lindsay 1999: 123).

Why is the US such a deeply religious society?

- The American churches have always had a voluntary, congregationalist character based upon the active participation of adherents. In contrast, the European churches were 'established' and had a legally protected position, tying them to government authority.
- There is intense competition between different churches and preachers. The churches have increasingly adopted marketing techniques so as to direct their message towards specific demographic groupings. They also offer 'bridge events', principally entertainment and social gatherings, that bring new members into the congregation.
- Christianity gained a hold among African-Americans during the years of slavery that continues to this day. It was one of the few forms of expression and organisation tolerated under the system of segregation that was subsequently imposed in the southern states. As Eugene Genovese records, faith held believers together: 'Christianity . . . preached the dignity and worth of the individual and therefore threatened to stimulate defiance to authority . . . The doctrine, "Render therefore unto Caesar the things which are Caesar's; and

unto God the things that are God's," is deceptively two-edged. If it calls for political submission to the powers that be, it also calls for militant defense of the freedom of the spirit and the autonomy of the personality' (Genovese 1976: 165).

- Many immigrants have strong religious ties. Roman Catholicism has been strengthened by immigrants from central and south America. Islam now claims about 3 million adherents. Furthermore, the churches traditionally provided a network of support for newcomers. Some, such as the Polish and Ukrainian churches in Chicago, also offered a means by which immigrant families could maintain an ethnic identity, but at the same time remain loyal to the US (van Elteren 1998: 56).

- Religious faith has been depicted as an attempt to find security and stability within a mobile, individualistic society. However, although influential, this theory has difficulties. While people resident in the states along the Pacific coast have the highest rates of mobility and fewest personal ties, religious affiliation is relatively low. In contrast, while the south has the lowest levels of mobility, religious affiliation is at its highest.

- Whereas more liberal churches allow 'free riders' who have invested little in their beliefs, the evangelical and fundamentalist denominations which are influential in the US require a significant degree of commitment from their adherents. This increases the value that individuals place upon membership (Neuhaus 2000).

Reasons

Why are Americans now 'bowling alone'? Putnam holds television primarily responsible. It not only takes up time, but it is also a privatised and largely solitary form of leisure activity. However, a number of other reasons can also be identified. These include the displacement of the corner store by distant and anonymous supermarkets and the growth of paid employment, particularly among women. The median number of hours of leisure each week has fallen from 26.2 in 1973 to 19.5 in 1997. Furthermore, the labour unions have lost members as traditional manufacturing industries declined. Similarly, the process of urban renewal destroyed long-established communities and networks. For their part, many conservatives stress the way in which the federal government has usurped the functions that were once undertaken by civil organisations. This claim is, however, countered by Theda Skocpol (1992) who stresses the part that government has historically played in developing voluntary efforts.

Others – particularly those associated with radical liberalism – share some of Putnam's thinking, but point to what they regard as the commodification of

American life and culture. Benjamin R. Barber ties his conception of McWorld (see p. 65) to the privatisation and commercialisation of civil society. Civic associations and communal forms of activity were edged out by the progressive enlargement of corporate interests and growing government interventionism. The federal government increasingly undertook functions such as charitable provision that had formerly been organised on a voluntary basis: 'Sqeezed between the warring realms of the two expanding monopolies, statist and corporate, civil society lost its preeminent place in American life. By the time of the two Roosevelts it had nearly vanished' (Barber 1996: 282).

To an extent, the populist Right shares this perspective. Its outlook is structured around representations of 'middle America'. These recall the small town, the sense of neighbourliness with which it was associated and the values to which it was tied. All of this, it is argued, has been undermined by the process of globalisation and the growth of the multinational corporation that has no allegiance to particular communities or nations. Patrick J. Buchanan, a former aide in both the Nixon and Reagan administrations, who campaigned to win the presidency in 1992, 1996 and 2000, emphasises the ways in which the multinational companies have used low wage labour in countries such as Mexico. This, he argues, has undermined American industry and the communities that depended upon it for employment and prosperity. He identifies himself, in particular, with the interests of American blue-collar workers: 'They did not need a course in global economics to understand what NAFTA [North American Free Trade Agreement] had done to their families and their field of dreams' (Buchanan 1998: 281).

Questioning Putnam

The arguments put forward by Putnam and his co-thinkers have not gone unchallenged. Some have asserted, for example, that although civic organisations have lost members, 'lifestyle enclaves' – based upon an interest, activities or a defining personal characteristic – have gained adherents. There are groupings – such as gay and lesbian organisations – associated with certain assertions of identity. Furthermore, large numbers have been drawn into charitable projects.

However, these arguments can be countered. In contrast with the traditional community, lifestyle enclaves are structured around one defining feature rather than the entire person. Furthermore, although some charitable events have attracted large numbers of participants, they often have a shallow character. In May 1986 Coca-Cola organised 'Hands Across America', the largest single participatory event in history (quoted in Rifkin 2000: 174). Four million took part and a further two million were involved in support events. However, as Jeremy Rifkin asserts: 'And when communities are no longer grounded in geography but rather defined by temporary, shared interests among people who interact with one another in virtual worlds, how does one retain any notion of collective solidarity and loyalty to place and country, long regarded as requisites for maintaining any sense of national cohesion?' (Rifkin 2000: 228).

For others, the internet serves as a mechanism by which close associations, relationships and ties are being rebuilt. Indeed, some have talked of 'electronic communities'. They point to the way in which e-mail allows frequent, informal contact that has undermined some of the customs and formalities inhibiting communication in traditional mediums such as the letter. Those with similar interests come together in user groups. Chat rooms facilitate intense bursts of contacts with both associates and strangers. Identities can be hidden, precluding discrimination on the basis of factors such as gender and race. As Harwood and McIntosh record: 'If Tonnies's *Gemeinschaft* exists on-line, it exists within e-mail, since e-mail creates a virtual bounded, yet non-spatial community. E-mailers bridge strong and intermediate ties with family, across vast distances, maintaining the ties of family and friends' (Harwood and McIntosh 2001: 12).

However, despite the promise of the internet, its ability to rebuild social connectedness should be questioned. Whilst e-mail encourages the communication of spontaneous thoughts and emotions, this can cut across the formation of relationships structured around trust and understanding. As Putnam notes: 'computer-mediated communication so lowers the threshold for voicing opinions that, like talk-radio, it may lead not to deliberation, but to din' (Putnam 2000: 173). The casualness the internet encourages – and the ease with which individuals can enter or leave 'cyberspace' – also prevents the construction of commitment and reciprocity. Moreover, like 'lifestyle enclaves', 'virtual communities' are formed around one form of identity such as a particular interest or affinity. Traditional communities, however, emerged around the totality of an individual's character. In addition, significant numbers – particularly those drawn from the minorities – are excluded from 'cyberspace' because they lack the income required for computer ownership. The term 'digital divide' has begun to enter the vocabulary.

Other criticisms of the civic decline thesis are perhaps on surer ground. Putnam's emphasis upon television as a primary cause of civic disengagement has been disputed. Pippa Norris argues that the claim is unproven, and TV news coverage may indeed contribute to interest and involvement outside the home. Furthermore, US participation levels remain relatively high compared with many other democratic nations (Norris 1996: 478–9). W. Lance Bennett suggests changes in the character of the labour market offer a more credible explanation of disengagement than television. Since the 1970s Americans, particularly women and African-Americans, have had to work longer hours and face greater job insecurity. Against this background, traditional forms of participation and organisations lost their former rationale (Bennett 1998: 752–8). Putnam's methodology and the overall coherence of his argument have also been questioned. How and why, it is asked, was the trust produced within voluntary groups generalised across society as a whole? Katha Pollitt asked in *The Nation* whether Putnam had picked on representative organisations. Many were, by the 1970s, already an anachronism:

> I've been a woman all my life, but I've never heard of the Federation of Women's Clubs. And what politically minded female, in 1996, would join the bland and matronly League of Women Voters, when she could volunteer with Planned Parenthood or NOW or Concerned Women of America, and shape the debate instead of merely keeping it polite? (Pollitt 1996)

There are also those who accept that civic decline may, as Putnam suggests, have taken place, but see his thesis as a nostalgic plea for a lost past. However, they ask whether the demise of the traditional community should necessarily be mourned. In the 1950s many communities were racially segregated and women had to assume most family, neighbourhood and communal responsibilities. At the same time, as Alejandro Portes and Patricia Landolt argue – and this has been reflected in films such as *Pleasantville* and *The Truman Show* – communities and close forms of civic solidarity rested on shared norms. There was little scope for personal autonomy or expressions of individualism: 'Membership in a community brings demands for conformity. The claustrophobia, however, may be asphyxiating to the individual spirit, which is why the more independent-minded have always sought to escape from these conditions and so much modern thought has celebrated the freedom of urban life' (Portes and Landolt 1999).

Furthermore, where there have been efforts to rebuild neighbourliness through the construction of 'gated communities', they have imposed significant restrictions upon the individual resident. Critics regard these as oppressive. David Brooks of *The Weekly Standard* regards some of the attempts to recreate civic solidarity as inherently authoritarian. As he asks: 'Do I want local busybodies with piddling township posts exercising their petty powers by looking into my affairs?' (quoted in Eberly 1998: 31). Many gated communities lay down rules specifying the colours homes are to be painted, noise limits and – in some instances – the types of dogs that may be kept as pets. This is significant because increasing large numbers live in these urban enclaves. In 2001 about eight million people were living in about 20,000 gated communities (*The Economist* 2001).

Projects and initiatives

Despite these criticisms, and the vigour with which they have been advanced, the civic decline argument struck a chord during the 1990s. It corresponded with a sense of concern, at least among intellectuals, politicians and columnists. Against this background, a number of projects took shape. Some of the initiatives pre-dated the publication of Putnam's article and others followed in its wake.

Some of the projects were scholarly in orientation. The Saguaro Seminar was established within the John F. Kennedy School of Government at Harvard University to publicise the initiatives and projects that would 'loosen America's hardened civic arteries'. Other initiatives were more broadly based. The National Commission on Civic Renewal was established. It was co-chaired by former Senator Sam Nunn, William Galston of the Democratic Leadership Council and William Bennett, who served as Secretary of Education in the Reagan administration and as 'drugs tzar' in the Bush White House. It drew up INCH – the Index of National Civic Health – a weighted index structured around twenty-two factors such as group membership, family life, political participation, trust, and crime rates, that sought to measure the decline of civil society. It showed a particularly sharp decline between 1984 and the early 1990s. In June 1998 the National Commission issued its report, *A Nation of Spectators*.

There were parallel initiatives. The Council on Civil Society – which included figures such as Francis Fukuyama as well as Cornel West, the radical black social commentator – also considered civic decline and also issued a report in 1998. The Heritage Foundation – a conservative policy research institute or think-tank – turned its attention to ways of rebuilding civic structures. Its journal, *Policy Review*, was relaunched for this purpose. In September 1995 Senator Dan Coats of Indiana established the Project for American Renewal. Its proposals included a call for a charity tax credit, allowing families to donate $1,000 of their tax bill to charities working within their own communities.

Some projects were initiated by the White House. Two years before Putnam had published his article, President Clinton and Congress established AmeriCorps. About 1,500 young people worked on sixteen community improvement and inner-city health projects, although the annual stipend that it paid led some critics to claim that it could not be regarded as volunteering. Then, in April 1997, the President joined together in Philadelphia with former presidents Carter and Bush, General Colin Powell, who served as Chairman of the Joint Chiefs of Staff during the Gulf War, and about 5,000 volunteers to promote the concept of community service. Powell announced that two million children would be helped through voluntary efforts by the year 2000. The gathering provided the basis for a national network, 'America's Promise'.

Divisions

Although the conclusions drawn about volunteerism should perhaps be qualified because certain projects offer financial rewards and a growing number of colleges require volunteering as a precondition for graduation, it is clear that a very wide range of activities and projects have been initiated. Some appear to have developed spontaneously as the 1980s and 1990s progressed. Others, particularly the nationally organised projects, were a response to the sense of crisis that Putnam's essay captured in the mid-1990s.

However, while the small, grassroots activities that were launched seem to have met with some success, initiatives such as the National Commission on Civic Renewal, the Council on Civil Society and the Project for American Renewal face difficulties and a question mark should be placed against their future. There is a split between those who regard the nation's crisis as civic and those who see it as moral. The National Commission on Civic Renewal talks primarily about the rebuilding of communities. In contrast, the Council on Civil Society stresses family values and the need for moral traditionalism. This, in turn, leads to markedly different sets of policy proposals. The National Commission emphasises neighbourhood projects that enable people 'to reclaim their streets and public spaces'. In contrast, the Council calls for programmes of pre-marriage counselling and stricter divorce laws.

There are also arguments about the proper role of government. Many of those on the Right – including George W. Bush – see a response to civic decline in terms of 'compassionate conservatism'. They stress the importance of building alternatives to government provision. Government interventionism has, they assert, sapped community-based effort. In contrast, those associated with liberalism and radicalism see government as a necessary counterpart to voluntary initiative. They also seek to extend civil society by placing curbs on the market. Benjamin Barber would take steps to turn shopping malls into public rather than private arenas. The internet would become a civic institution rather than a commercial opportunity. Workers' rights would be extended. He emphasises the importance of 'making corporations responsible'. There would, furthermore, be national and community service, and extended government backing for the arts (Barber 1998: 75). Putnam attempts to stake out ground for neo-liberalism, but he too favours government activism. The federal government should, he asserts, subsidise training programmes that bring together companies, educational institutions and community organisations. It should also consider the overall costs – in terms of social capital – of factory closures (Putnam 1993). Such thinking is an anathema to most conservatives.

Calls for the rebuilding of civil society have been widely endorsed because they appeal to both conservatives and liberals. Few will wish to oppose charities, volunteering or neighbourhood projects. For E. J. Dionne Jr of *The Washington Post*, these calls are the beginning of a 'new era of reform' (Dionne 1998: 13). However, the arguments that divide those involved in the civil society 'movement', once they progress beyond rhetoric and examine programmes and proposals, suggest that his optimism may be misplaced.

Education

Education was traditionally the responsibility of state and local boards of education. However, from the 1950s onwards, there was increasing national government intervention.

- The launching of *Sputnik* by the USSR in 1957 contributed to a crisis of national confidence and led to calls for educational reform and, in particular, the teaching of the applied sciences.
- Until the 1950s, education was segregated across the southern states. The process of desegregation depended upon rulings by the US Supreme Court, most notably *Brown* v. *Board of Education (Topeka, Kansas)* (1954), and the subsequent mobilisation of troops by President Eisenhower.
- Teacher shortages and inadequate facilities led the local school boards to seek increased levels of federal funding.

There is, nonetheless, doubt about the extent to which American public schools made overall progress during the latter half of the twentieth century. Studies suggest that although average scores rose in mathematics for seventeen-year-olds between 1971 and 1999, there was little improvement in average reading scores and those in the sciences declined (National Center for Education Statistics 2001a). Class sizes remain high in some states. In 1993–94, the average class size in Maine secondary schools was 18.5. In California, it was 29.7. Although there was a steady decline during the 1990s, violent crime remained a presence in some schools. In 1998, students aged twelve to eighteen were the victims of about 253,000 serious violent crimes such as rape, sexual assault and robbery. Between July 1997 and June 1998, there were forty-seven murders (National Center for Education Statistics 2001c). Although overall high school dropout rates – which were 27.2 per cent in 1960 – have declined, they remain disproportionately high among Latino and, to a lesser extent, African-American students.

During the 1980s and 1990s, fears about the future of US education and, in some instances, concerns about Supreme Court rulings that brought religious observance to an end in public schools, led to calls for school choice and the growth of the home-schooling movement. In spring 1999, an estimated 850,000 students aged five to seventeen, or 1.7 per cent of the student population, were being homeschooled. About a fifth of these were also part-time students in public or private schools (National Center for Education Statistics 2001b). Statistics suggest that children educated at home make greater progress – in terms of both reading and mathematics – than students attending either private or public schools. They surpass the national average in the major college entrance tests. However, home-schooling parents are not representative of the population as a whole. Of these parents, 81 per cent have studied beyond high school, compared with 63 per cent of parents nationally (Basham 2001).

Summary

Alongside individualism, individuals have traditionally had ties binding them to their families, neighbourhoods and the US itself. In an important study, *Bowling Alone*, Robert Putnam argues that there has been a process of civic disengagement. Some suggest that the decline of civil society has had cultural, political and economic consequences. In particular, it has given rise to hyperindividualism. However, although the disengagement thesis has been subject to a number of criticisms, it has encouraged the formation of civic renewal projects. Nevertheless, divisions among those working towards renewal may inhibit their efforts.

References and further reading

Almond, G. A. and S. Verba (1989), *The Civic Culture: Political Attitudes and Democracy in Five Nations*, Newbury Park, Sage Publications.

American Association for Higher Education (1995), *Bowling Alone: An Interview with Robert Putnam about America's Collapsing Civic Life*, muse.jhu.edu/demo/journal_of_democracy/v006/putnam.interview.html

Barber, B. R. (1996), *Jihad vs. McWorld: How Globalism and Tribalism are Reshaping the World*, New York, Ballantine Books.

Barber, B. R. (1998), *A Place for Us: How to Make Society and Democracy Strong*, New York, Hill & Wang.

Baritz, L. (1990), *The Good Life: The Meaning of Success for the American Middle Class*, New York, Harper & Row.

Basham, P. (2001), 'Home schooling: from the extreme to the mainstream', *Public Policy Sources No. 51*, Vancouver, Fraser Institute.

Bell, D. (1991), 'The "Hegelian secret": civil society and American exceptionalism', in B. E. Shafer (ed.), *Is America Different? A New Look at American Exceptionalism*, Oxford, Clarendon Press, 46–70.

Bellah, R. N., R. Madsen, W. M. Sullivan, A. Swidler and S. M. Tipton (1985), *Habits of the Heart: Individualism and Commitment in American Life*, Berkeley, University of California Press.

Bender, T. (1993), *Community and Social Change in America*, Baltimore, The Johns Hopkins University Press.

Bender, T. (1998), 'Community', in Wightman Fox, R. and J. T. Kloppenberg (eds), *A Companion to American Thought*, Malden, Blackwell.

Bennett, W. L. (1998), 'The uncivic culture: communication, identity, and the rise of lifestyle politics', *PS: Political Science and Politics*, 31:4, December, 740–61.

Buchanan P. J. (1998), *The Great Betrayal: How American Sovereignty and Social Justice are being Sacrificed to the Gods of the Global Economy*, Boston, Little, Brown & Company.

Carnoy, M. (2000), *Sustaining the New Economy: Work, Family and Community in the Information Age*, Cambridge, MA, Harvard University Press.

Derber, C. (1996), *The Wilding of America: How Greed and Violence are Eroding our Nation's Character*, New York, St Martin's Press.

Dionne, E.J. (1998), 'Introduction: why civil society? Why now?', in E. J. Dionne Jr (ed.), *Community Works: The Revival of Civil Society in America*, Washington DC, Brookings Institution Press, 1–14.

Eberly, D. E. (1998), *America's Promise: Civil Society and the Renewal of American Culture*, Lanham, Rowman and Littlefield.

The Economist (2001), 'America's new utopias', 1 September.

Fischer, C. S. (1992), 'Ambivalent communities: how Americans understand their localities', in A. Wolfe (ed.), *America at Century's End*, Berkeley, University of California Press, 79–90.

Fischer, D. H. (1991), *Albion's Seed: Four British Folkways in America*, New York, Oxford University Press.

Fogel, R. W. (2000), *The Fourth Great Awakening and the Future of Egalitarianism*, Chicago, University of Chicago Press.

Fukuyama, F. (1996), *Trust: The Social Virtues and the Creation of Prosperity*, London, Penguin.

Gallup, G. and D. M. Lindsay (1999), *Surveying the Religious Landscape: Trends in U.S. Beliefs*, Harrisburg, Morehouse Publishing.

General Social Survey (2001), *1972–2000 Cumulative Datafile*, csa.berkeley.edu:7502/cgi-bin12/hsda3

Genovese, E. D. (1976), *Roll, Jordan, Roll: The World the Slaves Made*, New York, Vintage Books.

Glendon, M. A. (1991). *Rights Talk: The Impoverishment of Political Discourse*, New York, The Free Press.

Harwood P. G. and W. V. McIntosh (2001), *Cyberspace: An Electronic Plymouth Rock*, Paper delivered to the annual meeting of the American Politics Group, 3–5 January.

Jasper, J. M. (2000), *Restless Nation: Starting Over in America*, Chicago, University of Chicago Press.

Ladd, E. C. (1999), *The Ladd Report*, New York, The Free Press.

Lasch, C. (1980), *The Culture of Narcissism: American Life in an Age of Diminishing Expectations*, New York, Warner Books.

Lemann, N. (1996), 'Kicking in groups', *The Atlantic Monthly*, April, www.theatlantic.com/issues/96apr/kicking/kicking.htm

Mahler, S. J. (1995), *American Dreaming: Immigrant Life on the Margins*, Princeton, Princeton University Press.

Murray, C. (1984), *Losing Ground: American Social Policy 1950–1980*, New York, BasicBooks.

National Center for Education Statistics (2001a), *NCES Fast Facts – Student Achievement (National)*, nces.ed.gov/fastfacts/display.asp?id=38

National Center for Education Statistics (2001b), *NCES Fast Facts – Home Schooling*, nces.ed.gov/fastfacts/display.asp?id=91

National Center for Education Statistics (2001c), *Indicators of School Crime and Safety, 2000 – Executive Summary*, nces.ed.gov/pubs2001/crime2000/

Neuhaus, R.J. (2000), 'Secularization in theory and fact', *First Things: A Monthly Journal of Religion and Public Life*, June, 86.

Norris, P. (1996), 'Does television erode social capital? A reply to Putnam', *PS: Political Science and Politics*, 28:3, September, 474–80.

PBS Online Backgrounders (1996), *American Exceptionalism*, 11 March, www.pbs.org/newshour/gergen/lipset.html

Pollitt, K. (1996), 'For whom the ball rolls', *The Nation*, www.thenation.com/issue/960415/0415poll.htm

Portes, A. and P. Landolt (1999), 'The downside of social capital', *The American Prospect*, May-June, www.prospect.orgarchives/26/26-cnt2.html

Putnam, R. D. (1993), 'The prosperous community: social capital and public life', *The American Prospect*, 13, Spring, www.prospect.org/archives/13/13putn.html

Putnam, R. D. (1995), 'Bowling alone: America's declining social capital', *Journal of Democracy*, January, 65–78, muse.jhu.edu/demo/journal_of_democracy/v006/putnam.html

Putnam, R. D. (2000), *Bowling Alone: The Collapse and Revival of American Community*, New York, Simon & Schuster.

Rifkin, J. (2000), *The Age of Access: The New Culture of Hypercapitalism, Where All of Life is a Paid-For Experience*, New York, Jeremy P. Tarcher.

Skocpol, T. (1992), *Protecting Soldiers and Mothers: The Political Origins of Social Policy in the United States*, Cambridge, MA, Belknap Press of Harvard University Press.

Smith, R. M. (1997), *Civic Ideals: Conflicting Ideals of Citizenship in US History*, New Haven, Yale University Press.

Stanley, H. W. and R. G. Niemi (2000), *Vital Statistics on American Politics: 2001–2002*, Washington DC, CQ Press.

Tocqueville, A. (1965), *Democracy in America*, London, Oxford University Press.

US Census Bureau (2000), *Statistical Abstract of the United States 2000*, Washington DC, US Census Bureau.

Van Elteren, M. (1998), 'The riddles of individualism and community in American and Dutch society', *Journal of American Culture*, 21:1, 43–80.

Wolfe, A. (1998), 'Is civil society obsolete?', in E. J. Dionne Jr (ed.), *Community Works: The Revival of Civil Society in America*, Washington DC, Brookings Institution Press, 17–23.

5

The family, sex and sexuality

Although – as Chapter 4 noted – the ethos of individualism shaped the character of American society, it has always been constrained by obligations, personal loyalties and 'bonds of affection'. The ties of family and kinship have a particular place in American iconography and culture. Holidays and celebrations such as Thanksgiving are, for example, closely associated with images of traditional family life.

Nonetheless, although representations of a 'traditional' family – structured around a male breadwinner and a wife who tended the home – have had a hold over the popular imagination, such images of family are rooted in particular historical moments. During the nineteenth century a significant proportion of households, particularly among the minorities, were female-headed. Many families took in relatives and lodgers. In working-class families, all had to work:

> Typically, a male laborer earned two-thirds of his family's income. The other third was earned by his wife and children. Many married women contributed to the working-class family economy by performing work that could be done in the home, such as embroidering, tailoring, or doing laundry, or caring for boarders or lodgers. The wages of children were particularly critical for a working-class family's standard of living. Children under the age of fifteen contributed 20 percent of the income of many working-class families. (Kellogg 1993)

Although rising real wages allowed increasing numbers to live in separate households and permitted women to stay at home, this was not to last. Family life was uprooted during the economic depression of the 1930s and during the Second World War (1941–45). During the war, many men served abroad in the armed forces while women were employed in traditionally male occupations such as shipbuilding. After the war, housing shortages compelled many couples to live with parents, relatives or friends.

It was only during the long economic boom of the 1950s and 1960s – and the sustained period of full employment that it brought in its wake – that the nuclear or conjugal family, structured around a father, mother and children, became the norm. Single living appeared deviant. By the end of the 1950s, 70 per cent of all women were married by the age of 24. On marriage, they were expected to relinquish paid employment and devote their time to domestic responsibilities and motherhood. During the 'baby boom', the birth rate doubled for third children and tripled for fourth children. Furthermore, although significant numbers of wartime marriages were dissolved, divorce rates stabilised in the 1950s. The nuclear family was partly a product of economic circumstances. However, as Stephanie Coontz has asserted, it also represented a form of both freedom and security:

> The 1950s was the first time that a majority of Americans could even *dream* of creating a secure oasis in their immediate nuclear families. There they could . . . escape the interference of an older generation of neighbors or relatives who tried to tell them how to run their lives and raise their kids . . . The private family also provided a refuge from the anxieties of the new nuclear age and the cold war. (Coontz 1997: 35–6)

Popular images of the American family should be qualified in another way. The American family is to some extent a function of ethnicity, race and income. Although the traditional 'privatised' family – structured around a male breadwinner and a wife responsible for the home – was a defining feature of white society, black family life has always had a different character. Some have portrayed this in negative terms. Indeed, since the mid-1960s, there have been persistent references to a 'crisis' in black family life. In 1965 Daniel Patrick Moynihan, at the time Assistant Secretary of Labor in Lyndon Johnson's administration, and later a US senator, wrote a report pointing to the large numbers of broken marriages, the 25 per cent of homes that were female-headed, and high levels of illegitimacy within the African-American communities. Moynihan asserted that there were historical reasons for this. The legacy of slavery and the cumulative effects of subsequent discrimination had, he said, placed many black men in a relatively weak position. They were unable to play a role as either husbands or providers and, as a consequence, many black families were unstable and had a matriarchal character (Rainwater and Yancey 1967: 76–7).

The report provoked savage criticism. Moynihan was accused of peddling racial stereotypes. His claim that the black family had been destroyed by slavery was challenged by Herbert Gutman who asserted that family life was relatively stable under slavery and during the great migration from the southern states to the northern states in the early decades of the twentieth century (Wilson 1987: 32). Other studies argued that black men did play an important familial role and also emphasised the positive features of the black family. In contrast with the white family, the black family appeared to have an extended character and ties with broader community networks. Carol Stack's 1974 survey of low-income black families pointed to co-operative familial arrangements. For example, 'aunts' and 'uncles' played a significant role in bringing up children (Bender 1993: 134–5).

Later studies appear to confirm the claim that family ties are weaker and family life is more 'privatised' within the white population. A 2001 study of people aged between 45 and 55 conducted for the American Association of Retired Persons (AARP) examined the extent to which their lives were organised around family responsibilities. It found that only 19 per cent of whites provided financial help or personal care for their parents, in-laws or other older relatives. In contrast, 28 per cent of African-Americans, 44 per cent of Latinos and 42 per cent of Asian-Americans give assistance (Lewin 2001). Furthermore, about a quarter of blacks and Latinos care for children other than their own, such as grandchildren, nephews, nieces and those belonging to neighbours.

Shifts and changes

Seemingly traditional representations of the family should, then, be placed in context. They owe much to the economic and cultural circumstances of the post-war era. Furthermore, from the 1950s onwards there were significant shifts and changes. By the 1990s less than 15 per cent of households were structured around the 'typical' family. Instead, there were significant numbers of working couples, single parents, stepfamilies, cohabitants and gay partnerships.

Table 5.1   *Percentage of men and women in the civilian labour force, 1960–99*

	Men	Women
1960	83.3	37.7
1970	79.7	43.3
1980	77.4	51.5
1990	76.1	57.5
1995	75.0	58.9
1999	74.7	60.0

Source: Adapted from Wright 2000:332.

How should these changes be explained? First, popular culture increasingly emphasised individual fulfilment and self-realisation. This incorporated a growing belief in greater sexual freedom. Second, although relatively few subscribed to radical feminist notions of marriage as an inherently patriarchal institution that – by definition – oppressed women, increasing numbers of women were no longer prepared to accept that they should be confined to a life structured around housework and childcare. They sought a degree of independence and an income of their own. Third, the increasing affluence of the boom years widened horizons and heightened the aspirations of those who were brought up during the period. Lastly, as the boom came to a close in the 1970s, real wage levels stagnated. Many wives and mothers were compelled to stay in work or seek employment. The overall proportion of working women rose to 60 per cent by 1999.

Table 5.2   *Women in selected occupations, 1975–2000 (proportion of total employed)*

	1975 (%)	1985 (%)	1995 (%)	2000 (%)
Auto mechanic	0.5	0.6	1.4	1.2
Bus driver	37.7	49.2	51.1	49.6
Computer systems analyst	14.8	28.0	28.5	29.2
Dentist	1.8	6.5	16.5	18.7
Economist	13.1	34.5	51.2	53.3
Waiter / waitress	91.1	84.0	77.4	76.7

Source: Adapted from Wright 2000:331 and Wright 2001:335.

Cultural and moral decline

Against this background, fears of moral and cultural decline became widespread. The conservative Right, in particular, asserted that family life was being destroyed. Robert Bork, whom President Reagan unsuccessfully nominated to the US Supreme Court, claimed that the US was 'slouching towards Gomorrah'. In 1994 William Bennett, who served as Secretary of Education and 'Drugs Tsar' in the Reagan and Bush administrations respectively, produced *The Index of Leading Cultural Indicators*. It charted what he termed the 'social decomposition' of the US. Bennett warned that 'unless these exploding social pathologies are reversed, they will lead to the decline and perhaps even to the fall of the American republic' (Bennett 1994: 8). He, and other conservative observers, cited the statistical evidence:

- The number of out-of-wedlock births rose from 5 per cent of all births in 1960 to 30 per cent in 1990. The figure reached 68 per cent among African-Americans in 1991.
- By the 1990s approximately half of all marriages were ending in divorce.
- The rate at which people were getting married was 25 per cent lower in 1990 than in 1960. Instead, many were opting for cohabitation or remaining single.
- More than 28 million abortions were carried out between 1972 and the early 1990s (Bennett 1994: 47–68).

Table 5.3   *Unmarried-couple households, 1960–2000*

1960	439,000
1970	523,000
1980	1,589,000
1990	2,856,000
1995	3,668,000
1998	4,236,000
1999	4,486,000
2000	4,736,000

Source: Adapted from Wright 2001:286.

Concern about the fate of the family was not confined only to those associated with the conservative Right. Cornel West, the radical black scholar, argued that the erosion of family relationships led to instability and insecurity. He joined with others in endorsing a platform that called for the reform of no-fault divorce laws, the promotion of 'covenant marriage' (see below), the favouring of married couples in the allocation of public housing, and the banning of school students who become pregnant (or father a child) from extracurricular activities or homecoming awards (Institute for American Values 1998: 19–20). Some **communitarians** – who want to see a shift away from individualism – have spoken in similar terms. William Galston, who served President Clinton as Deputy Assistant for Domestic Policy between 1993 and 1995, has condemned what he described as 'the easy relativism of the proposition that different family structures represent nothing more than "alternative life-styles"' (quoted in Ashbee 2001:516). Those who feared the consequences of civic decline have also been alarmed by the seeming disintegration of family life. In *Bowling Alone*, Robert Putnam charted the weakening of the threads binding family members together. He noted, for example, that the proportion of families usually eating dinner together had fallen from about a half in 1980 to 34 per cent at the end of the century. Other traditionally shared activities, such as vacations, attendance at religious services, or 'just sitting and talking' had also become individual pursuits (Putnam 2000: 100).

What – according to these accounts – had happened to the traditional family? In *Losing Ground*, Charles Murray (1984), an influential conservative commentator, suggests that welfare provision discouraged values such as self-reliance and personal restraint. Instead, it allowed young women to have babies without fear for the financial consequences. Women and men were no longer compelled to regulate their own behaviour. Myron Magnet, another conservative who later played a role in shaping President George W. Bush's faith-based charitable initiative, took issue with the proposition that human actions were simply a function of economic incentives and disincentives. Instead, he stressed the revolution in cultural attitudes that had been wrought by the 1960s. Student lifestyles had, he argued, permeated through society more generally. This had particular consequences for those in lower-income groups:

When middle class college kids began their fling with 'protest', drugs, sexual experimentation, and dropping out in the sixties, they had a margin of safety because of their class. Working class kids who today enlist under that washed-out banner, now demode, run a bigger risk. Once they drop out, some may never get back in. (Quoted in Ashbee 2000: 193)

Others pointed to the role of the mass media. Many films and television programmes, it was said, celebrated sexual promiscuity and portrayed 'alternative lifestyles' as morally equivalent to conventional family relationships. In a speech in San Francisco, Vice-President Dan Quayle castigated the television sitcom *Murphy Brown* for its positive portrayal of single parenthood: 'It doesn't help matters when prime-time TV has Murphy Brown – a character who supposedly epitomizes today's intelligent, highly paid, professional woman – mocking the importance of fathers by bearing a child alone and calling it just another "lifestyle choice"' (Carbone 1999). Other conservatives pointed to programmes such as *Roseanne*, *Ellen* and *NYPD Blue*.

For Cornel West and those associated with the radical Left, the decline of family life reflected the comercialised hedonism of the contemporary market economy. Young people, in particular, were being taught to disregard the values associated with traditional family life – such as caring and reciprocity – and think only in terms of material acquisition.

Remoralisation

For some, these trends were exacerbated during the 1990s. William Bennett (1998) regards the degree of support that President Clinton attracted during the 1998–99 impeachment crisis, and the apparent unwillingness of the American public to condemn his actions, as unambiguous evidence of declining moral standards. Despite this, however, others saw developments differently. They acknowledged that the 1990s could not be represented in terms of continuing moral decline, and that some of the cultural indicators that conservatives had cited at the beginning of the 1990s had changed in character as the decade progressed.

- The number of teenage pregnancies fell 19 per cent from an all-time high in 1991 to a record low in 1997 (National Center for Health Statistics 2001b). Alongside this, the teenage abortion rate dropped 33 per cent between 1988 and 1997 (National Center for Health Statistics 2001a). The overall number of abortions fell from 1,608,600 in 1990 to 1,365,700 in 1996 (Bennett 1999: 82).
- The divorce rate dropped from 1,182,000 in 1990 to 1,163,000 in 1997 (Bennett 1999: 69).
- Towards the end of the decade, there was a rise in the proportion of children

living in 'intact' families or two-parent, married couple homes. The rise extended across all demographic groupings. Between 1995 and 2000, the proportion of African-American children living in 'intact families' rose from 34.8 to 38.9 per cent (Blankenhorn 2001).

Table 5.4   *Marriages and divorces, 1945–99 (per 1,000 population)*

	Marriages	Divorces
1945	12.2	2.0
1960	8.5	2.2
1970	10.6	3.5
1980	10.0	4.8
1985	10.1	5.0
1990	9.8	4.7
1995	8.9	4.4
1998	8.4	4.2
1999	8.6	4.1

Source: Adapted from Wright 2001:281.

There is also evidence that, despite popular imagery, young people – sometimes dubbed 'Generation X' – are significantly more culturally conservative than the 'baby boomers' (those born in the aftermath of the Second World War and symbolised by President Clinton himself) were at a corresponding age (Leo 1999). As a consequence, there appears to be a growing sense of personal restraint at universities and colleges. Surveys of opinion among new students revealed, for example, that approval of casual sex fell from 51.9 per cent in 1987 to 39.6 per cent in 1998. This, the *National Catholic Reporter* noted, was a record low. There is further evidence of change. The True Love Waits urged young people to pledge 'to be sexually abstinent from this day until the day I enter a biblical marriage relationship'. In July 1994, 25,000 young people attended a rally that the campaign organised on the National Mall. According to figures published by the movement, a million students had accepted the pledge by the end of the decade. Others echoed the call for sexual restraint and fidelity. In October 1995 the Million Man March urged black men to rededicate themselves as responsible husbands and fathers. The Promise Keepers – the evangelical men's movement that attracted over 1.2 million to its rallies in 1996 alone – emphasised that the place of sex was within marriage. The third of the movement's seven promises bound adherents to 'sexual purity'; the fourth was a commitment to the building of 'strong marriages and families through love, protection and biblical values'.

In this climate, the Christian Right was able to win a significant legislative victory. In the 1996 Defense of Marriage Act, it gained broad backing for the assertion that homosexual relationships should not enjoy moral equality with heterosexual marriage. The Act – which was a response to judicial decisions and legislative moves in states such as Hawaii – defined marriage as a hetero-sexual institution. It sought to end moves towards same-sex marriages, pre-cluded gay couples from filing joint tax returns, and denied them access to spousal benefits under social security and other federal government pro-grammes. Although the debate in the House of Representatives Judiciary Committee had a largely partisan character, the House as a whole passed the bill by 342 to 67; in the Senate, only fourteen out of forty-six Democrats voted against it. President Clinton signed it into law.

At state level, there were moves to reform the laws allowing 'no fault' divorce. Such laws – first introduced in California in 1969 – are said to make divorce too easily available. By 1996 about forty states were considering legis-lation that would reintroduce notions of 'fault'. This would, according to David Blankenhorn of the Institute for American Values, a New York based think-tank committed to family restoration, 'communicate general attitudes that we take seriously, such as the idea that society cares whether a marriage lasts' (quoted in Ashbee 2001:515). Other state legislators have sought to establish 'covenant marriage' as an option for couples. This would be voluntary, but there are legal implications if a couple – who may either be engaged or wish to 'upgrade' an existing marriage – decide to take the 'supervows' that are

---

Gays and lesbians

The 2000 Census suggested that there was a dramatic increase in the number of same-sex couple households during the 1990s. In Vermont, for example, there was an increase from an estimated 370 in 1990 to 1,933 in 2000, a five-fold jump. Delaware saw a rise from an estimated 212 to 1,868 households, an almost nine-fold increase. However, most researchers attribute the increases to a greater willingness by individuals to identify themselves as gay rather than any big increase in such couples.

Table 5.5   *Homosexuality by race and age, 1998*

	Men %	Women %
Total	3.3	2.3
Whites	2.7	2.1
Blacks	5.3	1.8
18–29	3.5	2.6
30–9	3.6	2.1
40–9	2.8	2.5
50–9	2.4	0.8
60–9	1.9	1.4
70 and over	1.7	0.5

Source: Adapted from Wright 2000:298.

required. Louisiana, Arizona and Arkansas introduced covenant marriage in 1997, 1999 and 2001, although only small numbers have taken it up. If couples seek such a marriage, they must undergo premarital counselling and accept restrictions on the grounds for divorce; a marriage can be dissolved only if one partner is 'at fault' through, for example, adultery, abuse, or abandonment. The Arkansas law specifies 'cruel and barbarous treatment'. Furthermore, there is a waiting period of two years and compulsory counselling before a divorce can be finalised.

Limits and parameters

The scale of the changes during the 1990s should not, however, be exaggerated. There are limits and parameters. Only about 3 per cent of couples – generally drawn from those with church ties and in higher income groupings – have sought covenant marriage (Schemo 2001). The National Center for Health Statistics explains the fall in the teenage pregnancy, abortion and birth rates in terms of increased condom usage, the adoption of effective injectable and implant forms of contraception, as well as to changes in patterns of sexual activity (National Center for Health Statistics 2001b). Furthermore, a comparative study conducted by the Alan Guttmacher Institute and released in 2001 found that US teenagers were more likely to begin having sexual intercourse at a younger age – at about 15 – than those in England, Canada, France and Sweden. They were also more likely to have had multiple sexual partners (Wetzstein 2001).

Moreover, although there has been a shift towards traditionalism, many of the values promoted by the Christian Right have not been embraced. Organisations such as the Christian Coalition – which won a significant hold within the Republican Party during the 1990s – emphasise the importance of an orthodox family life structured around heterosexuality. However, the proportion of the population regarding homosexuality as 'an acceptable lifestyle' rose from 38 per cent in June 1992 to 50 per cent in February 1999. At the same time, the proportion of Americans condemning premarital sex has fallen. It was 36 per cent in 1972, but by 1996 had dropped to 24 per cent. Furthermore, the fall in the number of divorces can, at least in part, be attributed to the falling number of marriages. Instead, cohabitation between couples has become almost institutionalised. In 1960, for example, there were an estimated 439,000 households of couples living together. By the end of the century, there were 4.7 million. Furthermore, living together is now widely recognised as a formal relationship. In August 2000, 3,572 companies, colleges, universities, state and local governments offered or planned to offer domestic partner health insurance. Nor is cohabitation confined to the young. A 1998 survey suggested that 23 per cent of cohabiting couples were 45 or over (Gardyn 2000: 60–1).

Nonetheless, although the shift towards traditionalism should not be over-stated, it still requires explanation. Some commentators have seen the growing emphasis on fidelity within a particular relationship as a lagged reaction to the threat posed by the HIV virus and AIDS. However, a national survey conducted in 2001 for the National Campaign to Prevent Teen Pregnancy suggested sexually transmitted diseases were the most significant factor in holding them back from sexual activity. Federal government policy may also have played a role. The 1996 Welfare Reform Act included in its pro-visions bonus grants to the five states showing the greatest reductions in ille-gitimacy ratios. In schools, sex education programmes increasingly emphasised the importance of sexual abstinence. There has, however, also been a much broader and more generalised explanation of cultural trends. In his 1999 book *The Great Disruption*, Francis Fukuyama argues that the changes evident in the 1990s were an inevitable reassertion of moral tradi-tionalism. The 1960s – with its stress on personal and sexual 'liberation' and

Abortion

Although abortion remains a constitutional right – assured by the US Supreme Court's 1973 ruling in the case of *Roe* v. *Wade* – the individual states have imposed a number of restrictions. These include the imposition of waiting periods, limits on the use of public facilities, and conscience-based exemptions allowing medical personnel to opt out of abortions. Nine states have constitutionally unenforceable statutes requiring the notification of husbands. Although struck down by the Roe ruling, fifteen states still include a ban on abortion in their statute books. However, some states have adopted measures that assist women seeking an abor-tion. Fourteen states and Washington DC have laws protecting women and clinic employees from violence by 'pro-life' protestors. During 2000, seventeen states – including California, Illinois and New York – adopted 'pro-choice' legislative measures (NARAL 2001: xi–xii).

The number of abortions fell during the 1990s. Some attribute this to legal restrictions, the process of 'remoralisation', or the activities of pro-life organisa-tions. Others suggest, conversely, that the increased use of contraception played a role.

Table 5.6   *Reported abortions, 1990–97*

	1990	1995	1997
Abortions	1,429,577	1,210,883	1,184,758
Number per 1,000 live births	345	311	305
Proportion of women aged under 20	22.4	19.7	19.0

Source: Adapted from Wright 2001:374.

demands that constraints be removed – constituted an attempt to reject natural and rational ways of living. This, Fukuyama asserts, had very damaging implications for the individuals involved, those dependent upon them, and society generally. However, individuals are rational. They progressively understood the consequences of their actions and have begun to abandon the unrestrained individualism of earlier decades. They have returned to more traditional forms of living because these offer safety and security.

Summary

Although the traditional family – structured around a male breadwinner and a 'stay-at-home' mother – is sometimes represented as a social norm, it is instead a function of particular periods and circumstances. Furthermore, from the 1960s onwards, households have assumed an increasingly diverse range of forms. Established values have been challenged and some – particularly conservatives – have seen this in terms of moral decline. However, during the 1990s there appears to be a process of partial remoralisation. Although some forms of change have become institutionalised, social behaviour has had a more conservative character.

References and further reading

Alsop, R. J. (ed.) (1998), *The Wall Street Journal Almanac 1999*, New York, Ballantine Books.

Ashbee, E. (2000), '"Remoralization": American society and politics during the 1990s', *The Political Quarterly*, April, 192–201.

Ashbee, E. (2001), 'Marriage, the family and contemporary American politics', *Parliamentary Affairs*, 54:3, July, 509–25.

Bender, T. (1993) *Community and Social Change in America*, Baltimore, The Johns Hopkins University Press.

Bennett, W. J. (1994), *The Index of Leading Cultural Indicators*, New York, Touchstone.

Bennett, W. J. (1994), 'A strategy for transforming America's culture', *Vital Speeches*, 60:18, 1 July 1, 556–62.

Bennett, W. J. (1998), *The Death of Outrage: Bill Clinton and the Assault on American Ideals*, New York, The Free Press.

Blankenhorn, D. (2001), 'Is the family structure revolution over?', *American Values Reporter*, 10, October.

Carbone, L. A. (1999), 'Revisiting Murphy Brown: Dan Quayle was half-right, *Family Policy*, July-August, www.frc.org/papers/ familypolicy/index.cfm?arc= yes&get=fp99fd.

Coontz, S. (1997), *The Way We Really Are: Coming to Terms with America's Changing Families*, New York, BasicBooks.

Economic Report of the President (1999), February 1999.

The Economist (2000), 15 January.

Fukuyama, F. (1999), *The Great Disruption: Human Nature and the Reconstitution of Social Order*, New York, The Free Press.

Gardyn, R. (2000), 'Unmarried bliss', *American Demographics*, 22:12, December, 56–61.

Institute for American Values (1998), *A Call To Civil Society: Why Democracy Needs Moral Truths*, New York, Institute for American Values.

Kellogg, S. (1993), 'Family', *Encyclopedia of American Social History*, Charles Scribner's Sons; reproduced by the History Resource Center, Farmington Hills, Michigan: Gale Group, infotrac.galegroup.com

Leo, J. (1999), 'The joy of sexual values', *US News and World Report*, 1 March, 13.

Lewin, T. (2001), 'Report looks at a generation, and caring for young and old', *The New York Times*, 11 July, A10.

Murray, C. A. (1984), *Losing Ground – American Social Policy, 1950–1980*, New York, BasicBooks.

NARAL (2001), *Who Decides? A State-by-State Review of Abortion and Reproductive Rights 2001*.

National Campaign to Prevent Teen Pregnancy (2001), www.teenpregnancy.org/keeping.pdf

National Center for Health Statistics (2001a), *US Pregnancy Rate Lowest in Two Decades*, 11 February, www.cdc.gov/nchs/releases/00facts/trends.htm

National Center for Health Statistics (2001b), *Teen Pregnancy Rate Reaches a Record Low in 1997*, 12 June, www.cdc.gov/nchs/releases/01news/trendpreg.htm

Putnam, R. D. (2000), *Bowling Alone: The Collapse and Revival of American Community*, New York, Simon & Schuster.

Rainwater, L. and W. L. Yancey (1967), *The Moynihan Report and the Politics of Controversy; a Transaction Social Science and Public Policy Report. Including the full text of The Negro Family: The Case for National Action*, by Daniel Patrick Moynihan, Cambridge, MA, The MIT Press.

Schemo, D. J. (2001), 'In covenant marriage, forging ties that bind', *The New York Times*, 10 November.

Wetzstein, C. (2001), 'Study: US teen birthrates fall, but Europe does better', *Washington Times*, 29 November.

Wilson, W. J. (1987), *The Truly Disadvantaged: The Inner City, the Underclass, and Public Policy*, Chicago, University of Chicago Press.

Wright, J. W. (ed.) (2000), *The New York Times Almanac 2001*, New York, Penguin.

Wright, J. W. (ed.) (2001), *The New York Times Almanac 2002*, New York, Penguin.

6

Race, ethnicity
and 'Balkanisation'

Although there has been a process of change since the 1960s – when the southern states were compelled to abandon segregation – race and ethnicity are still defining cleavages in the US. Whites have a higher median income and are better placed in terms of socio-economic status. Furthermore, although there are shared values, there is also an attitudinal divide. Studies of television viewing suggest, for example, that blacks and whites watch different programmes. These differences have political consequences, and voting loyalties are in large part a function of ethnicity and race. Whites – particularly white men – disproportionately support the Republicans. In contrast, the minorities are drawn to the Democratic Party.

Race and ethnicity also constitute a basis for self-identity and group attachment. A 1995 study conducted in Los Angeles found that although 17 per cent of whites saw themselves as a member of a particular ethnic grouping as well as Americans, 54 per cent of blacks and 59 per cent of both Latinos and Asians chose a dual identity. Furthermore, although greater numbers subscribed to the 'melting pot' and believed that all should blend together, about a third of those who were asked wanted the different groupings to maintain a distinctive cultural character (Citrin 2001: 294–8).

African-Americans

The first Africans were brought to Virginia in 1619 when the crew of a Dutch ship sought provisions in exchange for a cargo of '23 and odd Negroes' (Campbell and Rice 1991: 2–3). Their status – and that of other Africans – was initially uncertain. However, from the 1660s onwards laws began to circumscribe their rights. While white indentured servants were freed after being bound to a master for a period between four and seven years, so as to pay the cost of their passage to America, blacks – and their children – were to remain the property of white masters for life. Although Enlightenment thinking and

Quaker theology led to the abolition of slavery in the northern states by the early nineteenth century, the southern economy was structured around cotton production and depended upon the use of slave labour.

The defeat of the southern Confederacy in the Civil War (1861–65) led to the abolition of slavery throughout the US. However, although African-Americans enjoyed a measure of political and legal equality during the **Reconstruction** years that followed the war, the ending of the northern military occupation in 1877 led to the progressive imposition of legalised – or *de jure* – segregation, dubbed the Jim Crow laws, across the South. These measures confined blacks to particular neighbourhoods and limited them to the most menial forms of manual labour. There was a small black middle class, but it was excluded from white society and the wider economy. Shopkeepers and other small business owners – who were restricted by law and starved of capital – served the black communities alone. At the same time, nearly all African-Americans were denied the right to vote, through a battery of arcane legal devices.

The Jim Crow laws, the poverty associated with the sharecropping system of agriculture, and the promise of industrial jobs led to millions of blacks moving towards the northern cities such as Chicago and Detroit. Thriving black communities were created, most notably Harlem in New York City. However, although the northern states were not segregated – and were sometimes hailed as the promised land – blacks still faced day-to-day discrimination and *de facto* segregation.

Against this background, protest movements began to emerge, although they had to take a clandestine form in the South. Some, most notably the National Association for the Advancement of Colored People (NAACP), which was formed in 1909 with the backing of white liberals, called for an end to discrimination. It cited the promises offered by the US Constitution and sought legal redress. Others emphasised 'race pride'. In the 1920s Marcus Garvey formed the United Negro Improvement Association (UNIA) and offered a powerful message to those living in Harlem and other black districts: 'Up you mighty race! . . . I am the equal of any white man; I want you to feel the same way. No more fear, no more cringing, no more sycophantic begging and pleading' (quoted in Jacoby 1998: 40).

In contrast with the NAACP's 'integrationist' message, early black nationalism rested on separatism. It looked towards the reclamation of Africa by blacks and also called for economic self-help within the African-American communities. It encouraged the formation of black businesses, and UNIA itself established groceries, laundries and a shipping line. At its peak, in 1923, UNIA claimed six million members. It proved difficult, however, to sustain black nationalism as an organised movement. Accusations of fraud were levied against UNIA's business ventures, and Garvey himself was imprisoned in 1925. Many within the African-American communities opposed Garvey's authoritarianism and his commitment to separatism. Indeed, UNIA was described by one critic as 'the Black Klan of America' (quoted in Marable 1985: 65).

Nonetheless, despite this, the idea of 'race pride' left an imprint. A new, assertive generation of black artists and writers emerged during the Harlem
Renaissance.

The tensions between 'integrationism' and black nationalism reappeared
forty years later. Martin Luther King and the civil rights movement of the
1950s and 1960s directed their efforts towards integration. They campaigned
against the Jim Crow laws and the denial of African-Americans' voting rights.
In contrast, the black nationalist Nation of Islam – associated with Elijah
Muhammed and, until his break with the organisation, Malcolm X – sought the
creation of a black nation on American soil. It emphasised dignity and self-help,
but also distanced itself from King's emphasis on non-violence.

The 1964 Civil Rights Act and the 1965 Voting Rights Act ended segregation and ensured that African-Americans could vote in the southern states.
These measures and federal court rulings brought the era of legal – or *de jure* –
discrimination to a close. However, profound inequalities remained. Although
a black professional class took shape and moved to the expanding suburbs,
black median income was still – in 1999 – only about 77 per cent of that for
whites. Furthermore, many of those who remained in the cities constituted an
increasingly separate **underclass** consisting of those locked into long-term
unemployment and poverty. Their lives, as William J. Wilson observes, were
characterised by 'social isolation' and a 'lack of contact or sustained interaction
with individuals and institutions that represent mainstream society' (Wilson
1987: 61). Furthermore, there are high levels of drug abuse and violence
among some groupings within the underclass. Indeed, homicide is the leading
cause of death for African-American men aged between fifteen and twenty-
four. For those aged twenty-five to forty-four, it accounts for more deaths than
heart disease, cancer or diabetes (Wickham 2001).

Latinos

Spanish-speaking – or Latino – settlements were established in the American
Southwest from 1609 onwards. In the centuries that followed, many Latinos
(or 'Hispanics') became Americans when the expansion of US led to the incorporation of territory across the continent. The 1950 Census recorded 9.1
million 'persons of Spanish surname' (US Census Bureau 1993: 2).

The Latino population grew dramatically over the half century that followed. This was largely because the immigration laws were reformed in 1965
so as to give preference to those with important employment skills and the
immediate relatives of those already living in the US. Although annual limits
are imposed upon the numbers admitted, and preference is given to immediate
family members, the introduction of family reunion as a basis for entry to the
US began a process of 'chain migration' from countries in Central and South
America. The number of Latinos living in the US grew by 58 per cent between

1990 and 2000. According to 2000 Census returns, there were 35.3 million Latinos and, although there were overlaps with other categories because Latinos can be of any race, they had overtaken African-Americans as the largest minority (Schmitt 2001).

However, although sometimes depicted as a homogeneous bloc, there are significant tensions and cleavages within the Latino communities. Indeed, some argue that the terms 'Latino' and 'Hispanic' are mere political creations and those labelled as such have few shared characteristics. From this perspective, ethnic solidarity is an artificial imposition. There are, they note, important differences among Latinos. Some of these are racial. As the US Census Bureau emphasises, some Hispanics are black while others are Asian or white. Many occupy different, and at times conflicting, identities. They 'cross racial and cultural lines between mainstream Anglos and the Latino community at work, in school, and in a variety of public institutions and settings on a daily basis' (Trueba 1999: xxxix–xl).

There are other differences. These are, in part, derived from countries of origin and the point at which the families of Latinos arrived in the US. Some, for example, can trace their roots back to the period before 1848 when the southwestern states were part of Mexico. However, others are newly arrived, or are descended from those who came to the US as immigrants from Mexico, El Salvador, Cuba and the other nations of Central and South America. Others are from Puerto Rico, but – because it is a US territory – are not counted as immigrants. In some areas, particularly the midwestern states, there are reports of bitter tensions between newly arrived immigrants and **Chicanos**, the Mexican-Americans who have been in the US for generations. Tensions have been fuelled by economic competition between the groupings, cultural stress and differential status. Many recent new migrants live in trailer parks on fringes of towns and are regarded as an underclass. At the same time, however, the new immigrants also look down on the Chicanos. They are seen as too Americanised. As one immigrant, living in Garden City, Kansas, commented: 'Chicanos may be his raza (race), but they're not his gente (people). Their heritage, he says, has been perverted by the more vulgar features of American culture – the lack of respect, the breakdown of family' (Campo-Flores 2000).

These economic differences have far-reaching implications. The 1990 Census revealed that among Cubans, many of whom live in Florida, 15.1 per cent were college graduates, over 7 per cent were self-employed and over half owned their own homes. In contrast, those from Puerto Rico – a US territory – have lagged far behind in terms of both educational attainment and income levels. Mexican-Americans fall in between these two groupings. Only 3.5 per cent were graduates, 4.5 per cent self-employed and only 36 per cent were homeowners (Trueba 1999: 36–7). There are also political divisions. Older Cuban-Americans have long been associated with anti-communism and the conservative Right. Other Latino groupings, however, lean towards the Democrats.

Nonetheless, despite these differences and cleavages, some suggest that there is a growing sense of Latino identity. Although there are many different dialects, about three-quarters of the Latino population speaks Spanish as their first or second language. They also share a religious faith; 70 per cent of Latinos are Roman Catholics and the family plays a significant part in everyday life. Despite disparities within the Latino communities, they are, furthermore, bound together by shared economic disadvantage. Although there are success stories, Latinos are disproportionately represented in the lowest income bands. In 1999 Latino median income was $15,262 compared with $22,012 for whites. Some of the poorest are concentrated in the **barrios** that have formed in many major cities.

Table 6.1   *Immigrants and countries of birth, 1998*

Mexico	131,575
China	36,884
India	36,482
Philippines	34,466
Dominican Republic	20,387
Vietnam	17,649
Cuba	17,375
Jamaica	15,146
El Salvador	14,590
Total from all countries	660,477

Source: Adapted from Wright 2001:296.

Asian-Pacific-Americans

The pioneers drawn to California in the 1848 gold rush included some from China. However, most Chinese migrants served as a reserve army of labour. About 12–14,000 worked on the construction of the transcontinental railroad in the 1860s. Others were hired as agricultural labourers along the west coast. A few, most notably in San Francisco, established themselves as entrepreneurs in the shoe, garment and cigar-making industries. In total, between the 1850s and 1880s about 322,000 Chinese immigrants arrived in the US. However, prejudice and the fears of the white working class led to the passage of the 1882 Chinese Exclusion Act (Lai 1980: 218).

Although the Chinese migrants were overwhelmingly male – often seeing themselves as **sojourners** who would return with their earnings to their home country – organisations, structured communities and **Chinatowns** emerged. Local stores not only sold goods, but also functioned as clubhouses, labour exchanges and banks. Clans and district associations – the **huiguan** – were formed upon the basis of surname or region of origin. The huiguan offered protection against outsiders, mediation in disputes and accommodation for new arrivals. Although challenged by secret societies, which were known in the US as **tongs**, they were the basis of social organisation in the Chinese comunities: 'An individual refusing allegiance to his huiguan would find himself stripped of protection and aid and faced with social ostracism, a practice that guaranteed the loyalty of a huiguan's constituents' (Lai 1980: 221). In 1882 the huiguan formed an umbrella organisation, the Chunghua Huiguan, which was also known as the Chinese Consolidated Benevolent Association.

While the Chinese communities remained largely distinct and separate in the decades that followed, there were shifts and changes. Although there continued to be a gender imbalance, women eventually gained entry to the US, providing a basis for family life. As Helen Zia, an Asian-American journalist who grew up in Newark during the 1950s recalls, it took a traditionalist form:

> In our household, it was understood that no one should ever disobey, contradict, or argue with the patriarch, who in the Confucian hierarchy is a stand-in for God. My mother, and of course the children, were expected to obey God absolutely. This system occasionally broke down when my mother and father quarreled, usually about my father's rigid expectations of us. But in the end, God always seemed to win. (Zia 2000: 11)

Some long-established attitudes were, however, diluted. The second generation allowed women to emerge from the home and accepted a degree of choice in marriage arrangements. Furthermore, the traditionalist conservatism of many community leaders was progressively undermined by the provision of government funding, allocated through the Johnson administration's War on Poverty scheme, opposition to the war in Vietnam, and the rapprochement between the US and China (Lai 1980: 230).

Although some Japanese workers were employed in Hawaii from 1868 onwards, most workers from Japan were brought to the American mainland to meet the labour needs of the Californian harvest in the 1890s. Many were indentured labourers who had to work for a period so as to pay off the cost of their passage. While there were distinctive Japanese communities in some cities such as San Francisco, and some families established a tradition by which one child – the *Kibei* – was sent to Japan to be educated, they adopted a more adaptive approach than many of the Chinese migrants. Rates of **out-marriage** were, for example, significantly higher. Japanese-Americans nonetheless faced comparable forms of discrimination. Although Amendment XIV to the Constitution ensured that those born in the US were citizens, first-generation immigrants could not become citizens until 1952. Furthermore, in California they faced legal restrictions on land ownership and were confined to three year leases. During the Second World War (1941–5), Japanese-Americans were regarded as a security risk and 120,000, 77,000 of whom were US citizens, were interned in desert camps. These conflicting pressures created profound personal dilemmas, particularly for the second generation or *Nisei*:

> The Nisei prior to World War II were in an untenable situation: they were not accepted by all as Americans and yet they were too thoroughly assimilated to feel themselves to be wholly Japanese. If they worked hard, they were seen as aggressive; if they did well in school, they were seen as too clever; if they attempted to join American organizations, they were accused of 'not knowing their place', but if they lived in comunities of their own, they were accused of being 'clannish'.
> (Kitano 1980: 565)

In the years that followed the war, Japanese-Americans made considerable economic progress. In particular, a new class of professionals emerged. In 1940 just 4 per cent of males held professional positions. By 1970 the figure had risen to 31 per cent. Japanese-Americans were no longer concentrated in urban 'Japantowns'. However, assimilation has been matched by countervailing trends. Further immigration and the creation of Japanese language television stations have contributed to the rebuilding of Japanese cultural forms and the reinvigoration of traditions that survived.

Others came from the Philippines. Like other immigrants, they joined the agricultural labour force in California. Many initially ventured overseas as sojourners and originally intended to return to their homeland. However, family pressures led many to stay. They 'sent dollars that could be used for purchasing land, paying taxes, financing the education of brothers or nephews, or fulfilling other obligations to the family system of alliances; the number of these obligations may well have been one reason why so many Filipinos stayed long beyond their original contract period – some never returned at all' (Melendy 1980: 357).

Whites

Although there were some settlers from other European countries such as the Netherlands and Germany, most of the early colonists were drawn from the British Isles. During the nineteenth and early twentieth centuries they were followed by waves of immigrants from across Europe (see Table 6.1). Despite the hopes of those who talked of the 'melting pot' (see pp. 4–7), the fears of cultural fragmentation that this aroused led to the passage of the 1924 Immigration Act. This brought nearly all immigration to a close for four decades.

As the twentieth century progressed, it was assumed by some observers that the defining features of ethnicity had been largely eroded and that the 'white ethnics', drawn principally from the countries of Eastern and Southern Europe, had been 'remade' as Americans. Nearly all the defining features of ethnic life seemed to live on only in literature and film. However, despite the assimilative

Table 6.2   *'White ethnic' ancestry, 2000 (US Census Bureau estimates)*

Czech	1,395,867
German	46,452,074
Hungarian	1,516,645
Irish	33,026,795
Lithuanian	714,729
Norwegian	4,547,291
Polish	9,050,122
Scots-Irish	5,223,468
Slovak	820,711
Swiss	996,671
Ukrainian	862,416

Source: Adapted from US Census Bureau 2001. US Census Bureau (2001).

process, ethnicity maintained a hold. Many remained 'hyphenated' and were 'Irish-Americans' or 'Italian-Americans'. Mike Royko has described Chicago in the 1950s:

> North of the loop was Germany. To the northwest Poland. To the west were Italy and Israel . . . Southwest were Bohemia and Lithuania. And to the south was Ireland . . . You could always tell what state you were in . . . by the odors of the food, the sound of the . . . language, and by whether a stranger hit you in the head with a rock. (Quoted in Morone 1996: 429)

The differences between communities were highlighted in the 1960s and 1970s by a series of studies. In *The Rise of the Unmeltable Ethnics*, Michael Novak maintained that there was a wide cultural gap between groups such as the Poles, Italians, Greeks and Slavs and the American mainstream. In such circumstances, there was no realistic prospect of adaptation and assimilation. The 'white ethnics' were 'unmeltable'. Although Nathan Glazer and Daniel Patrick Moynihan acknowledged – in their study of New York City – that the specifically national aspects of ethnicity did not usually survive beyond the third-generation of immigrants, they felt that the churches provided a basis for continuing subcultures and sub-communities (Glazer and Moynihan 1967: 313). In their opinion, the US remained a patchwork of different ethnic traditions: 'Individuals, in very considerable numbers to be sure, broke out of their mold, but the groups remained. The experience of Zangwill's hero and heroine was not general. The point about the melting pot is that it did not happen' (Glazer and Moynihan 1967: 290). Indeed, Glazer and Moynihan argued that there could even be a strengthening of ethnicity. They speculated that German ethnicity – which had been fragmented and lost during the wars – might re-appear in the years to come.

However, the assertions of those who emphasise the role of ethnicity as a cleavage among whites should be qualified and placed in context. For instance, from the nineteenth century onwards, the different 'white ethnic' groupings were bound together by race. They shared a consciousness of themselves as white, a belief that they were distinct from African-Americans, and a consequent sense of communality. David Roediger argues in *The Wages of Whiteness* that the Irish – whose 'whiteness' was initially contested – overcame the prejudice that they faced in the labour market by distancing themselves from the black population (Kazal 1995: 469). Theories of ethnicity also tend to neglect social class divisions among those sharing a similar ethnic background. Furthermore, the celebration of white ethnicity began in the 1960s as a conscious backlash against the civil rights movement and demands by African-Americans for economic and political advancement. This has led some to suggest that ethnicity is an inherently conservative concept (Kerber 1989: 423).

Despite the hold of ethnic consciousness, immigrants and their descendants have also had a sense of American identity. Indeed, many 'white ethnics' or 'hyphenated Americans' have long asserted that the Americanism to which they are committed is more authentic and they are more patriotic to the US than the WASP (White Anglo-Saxon Protestant) elites who are of English descent. These sentiments were evident during the McCarthyite campaign against communism in the years following the Second World War. Senator Joseph McCarthy was born into a family with Irish and German roots. Both his anti-communism and his sense of American nationalism were shaped by hostility to those in positions of authority, many of whom had English roots. These elites were, he argued, unrepresentative of, and disloyal to the American nation. Indeed, they had colluded with the Soviet Union.

At the end of twentieth century, survey evidence suggested that ethnic attachments had been eroded still further. A series of studies conducted in Los Angeles and across the country suggested that between 93 and 96 per cent of whites defined themselves – at least when first questioned – as 'just an American' (Citrin 2001: 295).

Illegal immigration

Figures from the 2000 Census suggest that the total number of 'undocumented aliens' (many of whom have overstayed the departure date specified on their visa rather than entered the US illegally) is at least seven million and possibly as high as eight million. The Center for Immigration Studies, a Washington-based anti-immigration think-tank, suggests that there was a net annual inflow of between 400,000 and 500,000 'illegals' per year during the 1990s (Cohn 2001).

Demographic shifts

During the 1980s and 1990s the differences between these racial and ethnic groupings were brought into sharper relief. Observers have pointed to the continuing gulf between black and white, the scale of Latino and Asian immigration, the shifting demography of the US and the apparent failure of the traditional mechanisms of assimilation. They draw, in particular, upon the projections compiled by the US Bureau of the Census. These suggest that the proportion of Hispanics or Latinos within the US population is growing dramatically. In 2000 they constituted 12.5 per cent of the population. By 2060, however, the figure will have reached 26.6 per cent. The Asian-American communities are set to grow – during the same period – from 3.6 per cent to 10.3 per cent. The predicted increase in the African-American population is of only marginal proportions, but it is expected to rise from 12.3 to about 14.8 per cent.

There is an inevitable corollary to these projections. The white share of the population (if white Hispanics are excluded), which constituted 69.1 per cent in 2000 will, by 2060, have fallen to 49.6. On the basis of this definition of 'white', the US will have ceased to have a white majority. California has already become the first of the contiguous states to 'fall'. Following on from this, as *The Economist* has reported, 'the transformation of minorities into a majority will, if present trends persist, slowly be repeated across the rest of the country: in Texas by about 2015, followed by Arizona, New York, Nevada, New Jersey and Maryland' (*The Economist* 1997).

There was also a process of fragmentation within the minority communities during the closing decades of the twentieth century. In particular, the overall composition of the Asian-Pacific-American population began to change. In 1970, for example, 96 per cent of Asian-Americans were Japanese, Chinese or Filipino. At the end of the 1990s, however, these groups constituted only about 50 per cent of Asian-Americans. The communities have been joined by sizeable numbers of Koreans, Vietnamese, Asian Indians, Cambodians, Pakistanis and Thais. They are mostly economic migrants, although many with a college education have been compelled to take low-status occupations on arrival in the US.

These demographic shifts are the consequence of increased immigration (see Table 6.2), differential birth rates and a slowdown in the overall rate of population growth. US immigration laws were amended in 1965 so as to end the system of numerical quotas that had, until then, restricted entry, particularly for those from outside Europe. In place of this, immigration policy was reformulated and based around the principle of family reunification. Those able to show family kinship with existing US residents were admitted. In the wake of the 1965 Act, the number of immigrants rose dramatically. Between 1991 and 1996 there were, for example, 6,146,213 legal immigrants. Furthermore, by 1996, a further five million people lived in the country illegally (Alsop 1998: 113–15). The consequences of immigration have, in turn, been magnified by a differential birth rate. Between 1990 and

Table 6.3   *Immigration, 1961–98*

1961–70	3,321,677
1971–80	4,493,314
1981–90	7,338,062
1991–8	7,605,066*

Note: * Includes more than two million aliens who entered or stayed in the country illegally, but were naturalised under the provisions of the 1986 Immigration Reform and Control Act.
Source: Adapted from Wright 2001:295.

1996 there were 106.3 births per thousand Latina women. The corresponding figure for whites was 65.6.

Balkanisation

The increasing diversity of the US became a recurrent theme in journals such as *The Atlantic Monthly*, and Peter Brimelow's book *Alien Nation* – a manifesto for those opposed to immigration (Brimelow 1996). Against this background, the term 'Balkanisation' became commonplace. It is, as Mark Ellis and Richard Wright record, 'a metaphor for ethnic antagonism, territorial disintegration, and societal malaise' (Ellis and Wright 1998: 688–9). In its most unrestrained form, it suggests that growing racial and ethnic divisions will eventually lead to secession from the US. Chilton Williamson, formerly Literary and Senior Editor at *National Review*, has for example raised the spectre of ***Reconquista***. He asserts that there will be attempts to pull southern California and neighbouring states away from the US: 'there has been talk in the Mexican-American community for at least two decades of using their numbers and the vote to effect the secession of several of the Southwestern states, which would either be incorporated by Mexico or form the new Nation of Aztlan' (Williamson n.d.: 114). The growing strength of separatist feeling in neighbouring Quebec, and predictions that the French-speaking province will eventually secede from Canada, has given such fears a degree of credibility.

Samuel Huntington of Harvard University does not cite secession as a danger, but he does assert that the national unity of the US will, with the erosion of a common culture, depend solely upon the degree to which Americans continue to believe in guiding principles such as individualism and equal representation. This, he asserts, is 'a much more fragile basis for unity than a national culture richly grounded in history. If . . . the consensus on liberal democracy disintegrates, the United States could join the Soviet Union on the ash heap of history' (Huntington 1997: 8–16).

Other well-known figures have talked in similar terms. Arthur Schlesinger Jr, the distinguished historian who served as an adviser to President Kennedy, has warned of 'the fragmentation, resegregation and tribalization of American life'

(Schlesinger 1992: 18). The novelist and essayist Gore Vidal has argued that 'only by force can we try to control a whole series of escalating race wars here at home, as well as the brisk occupation of the southern tier of the United States by those Hispanics from whom we stole land in 1847' (quoted in Nelson 1994: 119).

There are other, related claims. The attempts to hold the US together in the face of growing diversity may, it is said, lead the federal government to add still further to its powers. Furthermore, the Balkanisation process – and **multiculturalist** ideologies that celebrate rather than condemn diversity – have given credence to the concept of 'group rights' under which individuals are recruited to jobs, politically represented and judged under the law as members of a particular ethnic grouping. Such rights are seen by conservatives and some liberals as a negation of the principles of individualism and self-reliance upon which the US was founded.

There are foreign as well as domestic policy implications. It has been suggested that Balkanisation will increasingly lead to a process of 'finding or inventing enemies' so as to bind the country together. Benjamin Schwarz, reflecting on American actions in Bosnia, argues that contemporary US foreign policy has, in part, been shaped by ethnic and racial diversity in the US. It is an attempt to affirm that multi-ethnic states can survive and prosper despite their heterogeneity:

> The motivation behind this latest summons to a foreign-policy crusade, as with earlier summonses, lies not in external threats but in our own insecurities. These conflicts scare us because we see in them an image of ourselves . . . Afraid to face our own problems directly, we look elsewhere, and encourage other countries to prove to us that more pluralism and more tolerance are all that are needed to reunite divided societies. (Schwarz 1995: 67)

Residential 'segregation'

There are significant differences between the states and regions of the US (see Chapter 7). During the latter half of the twentieth century, 'gateway' cities such as Los Angeles, New York City, Houston, Miami and Chicago attracted large numbers of immigrants. Furthermore, while the suburbs were traditionally white preserves, the metropolitan regions that encircle the cities are now also acquiring a multi-ethnic and multiracial character. Although whites are now in a minority – or about to become a minority – within all these regions, each has a distinctive character. As William H. Frey records:

> The mix of ethnics differs in each of these regions: Cubans and other Caribbeans in Miami; Mexicans, Central Americans and Filipinos in Los Angeles; and a vast array of groups that have long been attracted to New York. The cities and suburbs in each of these melting pots will become similar, but one region will take on a dramatically different character than another. (Frey 1999)

At the same time, there has been a process of out-migration from these regions. During the 1990s more than four million people left the gateway cities and set up home in the 'heartland' regions. A significant proportion of these headed to the 'new sunbelt' states in the Southeast and Southwest. States such as Georgia and Tennessee have attracted large numbers. Others have sought out heartland states in the Rocky mountains and Midwest. These include Indiana, Wisconsin, South Dakota, and Nebraska.

Although some African-Americans have 'returned' to the southern states, the exodus has been overwhelmingly white in character. 700,000 whites left the state of New York alone. While some describe the process in terms of 'white flight' away from immigrant communities, William H. Frey suggests that white domestic migrants are instead seeking out jobs, natural amenities, family ties and an improved quality of life. Many are college graduates or retirees.

As a consequence of these processes, the US is – in terms of regional demography – two nations. It is divided between the metropolitan regions – which are both multi-ethnic and multiracial – and the remainder of the US, which is either almost entirely white, or, in the case of the southeastern states, biracial (white and black). By 2025 four states will have non-white majorities and eighteen will have non-white populations exceeding 40 per cent. However, in another twelve states, whites will constitute over 85 per cent of the population (Frey 1996: 758). Although the number of Latinos and Asian-Americans grew across the US during the 1990s, their numbers are a very small proportion of the overall population in the predominantly white, heartland regions. While, for example, the 2000 Census revealed a 20-per-cent growth rate among Latinos in Iowa since 1990, this still represents less than 3 per cent of the state population. Iowa remains 93 per cent white (Frey 2001a).

Frey describes the gateway cities as 'melting pots'. He argues that there will be increasing intermarriage between racial and ethnic groupings and a blending of cultures. However, projections such as these need to be approached with a degree of caution. Although the suburbs were once hailed as a vehicle for integration, there are significant spatial divisions – particularly between white society and blacks – across the metropolitan regions. The extent to which there is residential segregation in a particular area has been recorded in Karl Taeuber's **dissimilarity** index (Ashbee 2000:11). A score of 1.00 indicates the total physical separation between groupings. A score of 0.00 indicates total integration. In cities such as Detroit (0.88) and Cleveland (0.85), a large majority of whites and blacks live in separate neighbourhoods. Although it takes a less severe form, Latinos are also subject to residential segregation. The New York dissimilarity index for Latinos is 0.66. In Newark, the figure is 0.67. Although more integrated, many Asian-Americans also live in largely separate neighbourhoods. The dissimilarity index reveals a figure of 0.51 for Buffalo in upstate New York.

A study of Los Angeles County drew similar conclusions. Although there was some mixing between whites and Latinos, whites and blacks continued to live apart. In 1940 whites in LA County had a 1-per-cent chance of having a black neighbour. By 2000 the figure had only risen to 5 per cent. Although some African-Americans are moving to the suburbs, they are living in those sections of the suburbs that have less desirable schools, fewer employment opportunities and a declining tax base, which will preclude spending projects in the future (Fields 2001). Furthermore, the 2000 Census suggested that the degree of separation between Latinos, Asian-Americans and other groupings during the 1990s had become more pronounced. When the figures for 1990 and 2000 were compared, Latinos and Asians were more likely to live separately in nineteen and twenty-one of twenty-five metropolitan areas respectively (Fields and Herndons 2001).

Language

The Balkanisation thesis rests on the assertion that there are significant cultural differences between immigrant groupings and the established population of the US. Some have argued that the country is becoming a 'tower of Babel' in

Affirmative action

The attitudinal divide between the different races and ethnic groupings is evident in opinions about affirmative action. This is the adoption of measures intended to ensure that minorities and women are much more fully represented in traditionally male occupations. In its 'soft' form, it involves the use of job advertisements in the minority press and other initiatives designed to increase the number of minority applicants for particular posts. In its 'hard' form, affirmative action involves the adoption of quotas so that minority applicants are given preference over white men. To some extent, poll responses depend upon the form of words that are used and the form of affirmative action that appears to be under consideration.

Table 6.4   *Attitudes towards affirmative action in California, 1998–2000*

	Ended now	Phased out	Continued	N
White	33	39	27	*1132*
Black	4	19	78	*111*
Latino	13	21	66	*458*
Asian	19	32	49	*86*

Note: The findings are based on an aggregation of surveys conducted between April 1998 and May 2000.

Source: Adapted from Hajnal and Baldassare 2001:15.

which a multitude of languages is spoken. According to the 1990 Census, 329 different languages are being used. An estimated thirty-two million Americans speak a language other than English at home. The 1990 Census suggested that 56 per cent of Asian-Americans aged five or over did not speak English 'very well' and 35 per cent were 'linguistically isolated' (US Census Bureau 1999: 5). *Univision*, the leading Spanish-language television station, is now the fifth largest television network in the US.

By 2050, according to projections, over twenty-one million American residents will be unable to speak English. Interest groups such as US English suggest that this threatens the coherence and integrity of the nation. English, they assert, provides 'a common reference point that bonds all citizens'. The use of English is, the organisation asserts, 'crucial . . . to our national unity' (Ashbee 2000:13). It campaigns to establish English as the official language of government and seeks to ensure that immigrants learn the language at the earliest opportunity.

The attitudinal divide

There are also differences of attitude and belief. Those who talk of Balkanisation have resurrected fears that were evident a hundred years earlier and emphasise the assertion that many within the minorities define themselves in terms of their country of origin rather than as Americans. Others maintain ethnic attachments that cut across national loyalty. The *Latino Ethnic Attitude Survey* indicated that 72 per cent of Latinos regarded ethnicity as 'very important' in defining their personal identity and a further 21 per cent defined it as being 'somewhat important' (Roy 1999).

Furthermore, although there have been suggestions that, with the passage of time, minorities will be progressively assimilated into the American mainstream, survey evidence reveals that the grandchildren and great-grandchildren of Mexican immigrants in low-income groups are consciously rejecting the assimilation process. De la Garza, Falcon, Garcia and Garcia surveyed levels of support for 'core' American values and the learning of the English language among those in low-income groups. They found that although the ideology of Americanism was widely endorsed, resistance was highest among fourth-generation immigrants. They conclude that 'increased exposure to American society, as indicated by deeper generational roots in American society, tends to be inversely associated with support for core values' (De la Garza, Falcon, Garcia and Garcia 1994: 248). They attribute this to a lack of social and economic mobility.

The differences are also evident in terms of religious faith. Although Latino immigration has led to a reinvigoration of Catholicism, Islam has also gained a hold. By 1998 between six and eight million Americans, about a quarter of whom were black, were Muslims. Muslims now outnumber Presbyterians,

Episcopalians and Mormons. The city of Houston has twenty five mosques and four Islamic schools.

Furthermore, the children and grandchildren of immigrants have remained separate and distinct. Indeed, in some ways, the gulf between minorities and white society has widened: 'Many . . . responded to their perceived lack of opportunity and to their rejection at the hands of nativist whites by constructing what are now called "reactive identities", identities premised upon value schemes that invert those of the mainstream in important ways' (Alba and Nee 1997; 848).

The black middle class

The black middle class grew in size and changed in character from the 1960s onwards. Under segregation and the less institutionalised forms of discrimination pursued in the northern states, the black middle class was tied to a limited number of professions and undercapitalised forms of small-scale entrepreneurship. Although, as E. Franklin Frazier suggests (1965), it attempted to ape the social mannerisms of white society, it was, in reality, unable to escape the confines of racism.

Since then, the black middle class has expanded. Furthermore, increasing numbers have been employed in management positions by companies and – to a greater extent – in the public sector. Living standards have risen significantly. However, studies suggest that far from being progressively absorbed into the political mainstream, a significant gulf remains. Whereas middle-income whites have a deeply rooted faith in the 'American dream' – and believe in the US's ability to offer material rewards to those who strive – there is evidence among blacks of an inverse relationship between affluence and commitment to the dream. Despite relative prosperity, and a high level of personal optimism, the black middle class does not appear to share the belief that US society offers a reasonable prospect of material reward to individuals who work hard and take risks. Although she is also struck by its resilience, Jennifer Hochschild has charted the growing disillusionment with the American dream: 'By the 1990s well-off blacks have come to doubt the reality of the dream for African-Americans. They have also become increasingly pessimistic about the future of the dream in general, and more embittered about American society than white Americans expect' (Hochschild 1995: 87).

Ellis Cose has taken this a stage further by speaking of black middle class 'rage'. He argues that living standards have only increased to a limited extent. Many African-Americans are confined to the underclass and those who have climbed the income ladder have made only partial gains. Black-owned businesses are limited in terms of size, scope and capital. If the top thousand black businesses were merged into one, it would only be the eighty-third largest US corporation when ranked by revenue (*CQ Researcher* 1998b: 64). White America has broken its 'covenant' with blacks. It offered an assurance that if they worked hard, they could share the American dream. Cose asserts, however, that the promise has not been realised.

The continuing gulf between blacks and whites has political consequences. Despite material progress, African-Americans have been the Democrats' most loyal constituency since the presidential election of 1964. The degree of support for the party was evident in the November 1998 mid-term elections when 88 per cent of black voters supported Democratic candidates. It can also be seen in terms of ideas. There is, within the black communities, a deeply rooted suspicion and hostility towards the wider world. This is reflected in conspiracy theories, many of which have established a tenacious hold. A large proportion of these rest upon the belief that government agencies and white institutions are, quite literally, seeking black genocide. A 1990 *New York Times/CBS News* poll of black New Yorkers found that 29 per cent felt that it was either true or 'possibly true' that AIDS 'was deliberately created in a laboratory in order to infect black people'. Furthermore, 40 per cent of black college students in Washington DC stated that they believed that the HIV virus had been manufactured in a germ-warfare laboratory. Other widely held beliefs include the claim that black men are being sterilised by contaminated food (Ashbee 2000:15).

Political differences

Set against African-Americans who have been overwhelmingly loyal to the Democrats from 1964 onwards, other minorities were, until the 1990s, more equivocal. Both Richard Nixon and Ronald Reagan attracted about a third of the Latino vote. However, in 1992 and 1996 George Bush and Bob Dole won only a 24-per-cent and 20-per-cent share respectively. The reasons for the decline in Latino support for the Republicans appear to lie in its growing identification with notions of minority status and in fears about the Republican Party's identification with particular legislative proposals. In California, there were Republican-backed campaigns to withdraw state benefits from illegal immigrants and end affirmative action. These led to the passage of Propositions 187 and 209. Although a sizeable minority of Latinos supported both measures, they had symbolic significance and were successfully portrayed as anti-Hispanic. They contributed to a rise in registration, turnout and support for the Democratic Party among Latinos.

There have also been shifts within the Asian-American communities. Traditionally, the Republicans won a majority of their vote, albeit against a background of a low turnout. Asian-Americans were hailed as the 'model minority', and were associated with anti-communism, entrepreneurial values, close-knit family structures and the work ethic. However, as the 1990s progressed, increasing numbers of Asian voters joined the Democratic camp. The Republican share of the Asian presidential vote slipped between 1992 and 1996 from 55 per cent to 48 per cent. By 1998 it had fallen to 42 per cent. The shift can, in part, be attributed to the changing character of the Asian communities. Memories of communism, which appear to have drawn refugees towards the Republican Party during the Cold War years, may have faded. Although there are high average levels of education and income within the Asian-American communities, more recent immigrants have been relatively poor. Activists reinterpreted the Asian-American experience so as to cast themselves as members of a homogeneous minority. Furthermore, some Republican strategies and tactics backfired. Congressional inquiries into 1996 election fund-raising appeared to have anti-Asian implications. The Party's criticisms of Bill Lann Lee, who was appointed by President Clinton to serve as Assistant Attorney-General for Civil Rights, were – paradoxically because Lee has backed affirmative action programmes that at times restricted educational and employment opportunities for Asian-Americans – seen as a rebuttal of Asian political ambitions.

The scale of backing for the Democrats among the minorities has led to forecasts of a significant political shift. As Zoltan Hajnal and Mark Baldassare note: 'Indeed, California could, over time, take on the character of a one-party dominant state if current registration patterns among newly registering Latinos and Asian Americans continue' (Hajnal and Baldassare 2001: 61). Peter Brimelow and Ed Rubenstein of *National Review* go beyond this and talk of the demise of the Republican Party and long-term Democratic hegemony. The minorities are, they suggest – as the 'pork barrel' beneficiaries of federal assistance – tied to 'big government'. This draws them to the Democrats, who can still claim the allegiance of a core white vote. Changing demography means that it will be impossible for the Republicans – who are seen as the party of 'small government' – to win presidential elections after 2004 (Brimelow and Rubenstein 1997: 32).

The demise of the melting pot

Those who talk of Balkanisation cite a past in which the traditional mechanisms, such as intermarriage, schools and the demands of the workplace, ensured that assimilation took place. They look back to an era structured around the 'melting pot'. Although they acknowledge that there are, in some cases, group-specific reasons why cultural assimilation has been limited, they also suggest that the causes of Balkanisation lie in the character of contemporary immigration and the abandonment of the melting pot. They point, in particular, to the weight of immigrant numbers. As Glynn Custred, a professor of anthropology and co-founder of the campaign to secure the passage of Proposition 209 – which brought state affirmative action programmes to an end in California – puts it, 'high immigration fosters ethnic enclaves in which immigrants retain their original language and culture'(Custred 1997: 40). The growing size of the Latino communities has also made intermarriage more unusual. In 1990, for example, only 6 per cent of foreign-born Hispanic men were married to non-Hispanics.

The geographical proximity of Central America and the changes brought about by air travel also play a part. Today's immigrants have maintained ties with their country of origin, whereas earlier generations were forced by circumstances to break their associations with Europe. Others argue that the process of 'making it' in the US originally required **Americanisation**. This, they say, is no longer the case. The growth of affirmative action programmes and other forms of race-based policy making have created perverse incentives. Personal advancement – particularly in higher education and professional employment – increasingly rests on individuals' identification with particular minority cultures, rather than the extent to which they have been incorporated within the cultural 'mainstream'.

There have also been suggestions that the schools have undermined the integrity of the nation. Critics assert that the teaching of multiculturalism and the celebration of minority traditions rather than US national values have weakened patriotic identity. There is some empirical confirmation of this. A study of San Diego school students conducted between 1992 and 1995 suggested that three years of high school led to a significant decline in the numbers defining themselves as American or as 'hyphenated Americans' and a 52 per cent increase in those describing themselves exclusively in terms of their original identity (Ashbee 2000: 17–18).

Multiculturalism

Although the term 'Balkanisation' is the property of those who fear the crumbling of the American nation and state, the assertion of group rights, growing cultural diversity, and the recognition of the US as a multi-ethnic state has, at times, been represented in another way. Less than a decade after Israel Zangwill's play had established the 'melting pot' to the national vocabulary, Horace Kallen made a plea for a different understanding of America. Writing in *The Nation* in February 1915, he called for the US to celebrate its differences and reconstitute itself as a 'federation of nationalities'. He called for 'cultural pluralism'. Although he cast aside black interests, Kallen wanted to allow ethnic groupings to retain their own cultural traditions within the overall framework of a unified country. He sought assimilation 'in matters economic and political', dissimilation 'in cultural consciousness' (Walzer 1996: 37). The US would become:

> A democracy of nationalities, cooperating voluntarily and autonomously through common institutions . . . The common language of the commonwealth would be English, but each nationality would have for its emotional and involuntary life its own peculiar dialect or speech, its own individual and inevitable esthetic and intellectual forms. (Quoted in Gleason 1982: 97)

The ideas re-emerged in the closing decades of the twentieth century. Contemporary multiculturalism echoes Kallen's approach but, in many of its forms, gives it a more polemical edge by depicting the US as an imperialist power and asserting that traditional representations of the American nation have masked the hegemony of a white Anglo-Saxon elite. As Amiri Baraka, the African-American poet and playwright puts it, 'the Eurocentric construct of so-called official Western culture, America is a racist fraud' (Baraka 1998: 392).

Multiculturalist thinking has – as noted above – taken root within the American classroom. In 1989 the New York State Commissioner of Education, Thomas Sobol, issued a 'Curriculum of Inclusion'. Nathan Glazer, a veteran neoconservative, argues that schooling has been changed irreversibly: 'Those few who want to return American education to a period in which the various subcultures were ignored, and in which America was presented as the peak and end-product of civilization, cannot expect to make any progress in the schools' (quoted in Berube 1997). There have also been attempts to build on multiculturalism by recognising black English or 'Ebonics' – a fusion of the words 'ebony' and 'phonics' – as a legitimately separate language. Although the efforts were later abandoned, following public controversy, the Oakland (California) school board voted in December 1996 to apply for bilingual education funding so that teachers could be given appropriate training.

However, the philosophy of multiculturalism extends beyond education. Lani Guinier asserts that political structures should be reformed so as to represent collective ethnic and racial identities as well as the individual citizen. Guinier was nominated in early 1993 as Assistant Attorney General responsible for the Civil Rights Division. Her nomination was, however, withdrawn by President Clinton following press criticisms of her as a 'quota queen'. In Guinier's view, recalling the words of James Madison, blacks suffer from the 'tyranny of the majority'. Under a winner-takes-all voting system, and in a racially polarised society such as the US, minority candidates can be permanently excluded from public office: 'The problem is that majoritarian systems do not necessarily create winners who share in power. Politics becomes a battle for total victory rather than a method of governing open to all significant groups' (Guinier 1994: 10).

Although Guinier has held back from endorsing specific measures, she argues that some forms of decision making should require a 'supermajority' rather than a simple plurality of votes. She also suggests that cumulative voting systems should be considered. These would rest on multimember constituencies and voters would have as many votes as there were representatives for that district. Although racial bloc voting could continue, a minority could, at the same time, concentrate its vote so as to ensure that at least one of its nominees was elected: 'any self-identified minority can plump or cumulate all its votes for one candidate'.

Corporate interests

Multiculturalist thinking is popularly associated with the issue-advocacy organisations of the Left. However, affirmative action and 'diversity management' have been pursued with increasing vigour by industry and commerce.

Affirmative action – whereby particular efforts are made to ensure the composition of the workforce is broadly representative of American society – is now
an established feature of corporate life. It has been endorsed, for example, by the
National Association of Manufacturers and the Equal Employment Advisory
Council, which includes most of the Fortune 300 companies.

As the 1990s progressed, many companies sought to progress beyond affirmative action policies. They took their commitment to multiculturalist thinking a stage further by beginning to talk about 'managing diversity'. Whereas
affirmative action policies seek only to change recruitment strategies, diversity
programmes attempt to transform the entire company atmosphere and structure. They are intended to ensure that companies are reorganised around the
values and norms of minorities as well as the majority. Every aspect of company
life is assessed so as to judge its impact on minority employees.

Such programmes have won a degree of boardroom backing for five principal reasons. First, there is a growing recognition that because of differential
population growth rates, the Latino market has, in particular, become pivotal.
By 2001 one estimate suggested that it was worth $500 billion. Demographers
have, furthermore, pointed to the expansion of the Latino middle class and predicted that the number of Latinos who are aged eighteen to forty-nine, a core
spending group, will grow by 27 per cent between 2000 and 2010, a rate far
outpacing the general population (Johnson 2001). As a senior manager put it:
'If you don't try to market to them, you're not going to get a share of that
growth'.

Second, diversity management will, it is said, assist corporate efforts to
recruit the brightest and best from a workforce that is increasingly drawn from
the minorities. As James Preston, chairman and CEO of Avon cosmetics puts it:
'If you're going to attract the very best of these people, then they had better
believe that your organization has an environment in which they can prosper
on the basis of their performance, regardless of their ethnicity, religion, background or accents' (*Institutional Investor* 1995: 21). At the same time, by
reducing workplace alienation, diversity management enables companies to
cut down turnover and absenteeism levels, thereby leading to overall cost
savings.

Furthermore, proponents of diversity management suggest that companies

Assimilation questioned

Some on the conservative Right have begun to question assimilationism as a
policy objective. Many immigrants, they argue, are drawn from traditional communities that attach importance to hard work and family integrity. Such values
have, however, been undermined by the debased values of contemporary
American society (Renshon 2001: 8).

gain by employing culturally heterogeneous teams. Such companies understand the needs of different domestic and overseas markets. They will also
produce more innovative solutions to commercial problems than teams characterised by uniformity. Lastly, companies will be able to learn from the cultural perspectives offered by minorities and women, and tap their creativity.
Diversity training emphasises how in the post-war era other nations and cultures, using different approaches, have had more economic success – particularly in terms of productivity growth – than the US.

The assimilationist response

The claims of those who talk of Balkanisation and multiculturalism have,
however, been countered. Significant numbers of observers emphasise the
degree to which there has been **assimilation** and the capacity of the contemporary US to draw in and 'Americanise' newcomers. While some stress the importance of structural assimilation – the point at which minorities begin to
establish primary group relationships with the majority community – most
stress attitudinal change. They define assimilation as a process in which individuals acquire the folkways and attitudes of another grouping and are thereby
incorporated into a common cultural life.

The assimilationist camp – which has backers among both conservatives
and liberals – emphasises sameness and homogeneity. From this perspective,
Americans – regardless of race and ethnicity – consume the same products,
watch many of the same television shows and share similar material goals.
Furthermore, the assimilationist argument asserts that the country is moving
towards ethnic and racial peace rather than war and that those who emphasise
division and cleavage are guilty of hyperbole. Stephan and Abigail
Thernstrom's 1997 study, *America in Black and White* is representative. They
argue that, despite inequalities and tensions, the US remains, in the words of
the book's subtitle, *One Nation, Indivisible*.

Those who talk in terms of assimilationism put forward several principal
arguments. First, the demographic projections – which show a rapid growth in
the Latino population – may be proved wrong. In the past, population predictions have often been mistaken. The baby boom that followed the Second World
War was, for example, unexpected. Furthermore, although current Latino
birth rates are still closer to those in parents' country of origin, they may well
fall over successive generations. The claim that there are spatial divisions
between racial and ethnic groupings – sometimes still described as 'segregation'
– has also been challenged. Although criticised for taking an unrepresentative
sample, a study by the Brookings Institution concluded that 272 of the
country's 291 metropolitan areas had become more integrated during the
1990s. Change was most evident, it argued, in the South and West (Fields
2001).

Those who assert that there has been a process of assimilationism also argue that white attitudes have changed since the segregationist era, and prejudice against minorities has been largely delegitimised. Stephan and Abigail Thernstrom stress that a majority of both blacks and whites are now committed to integration. Patterns of social interaction reflect this. In 1964 only 18 per cent of whites reported having a black friend. By 1989 it had risen to about two-thirds. Other studies confirm these findings. In 1958 only 35 per cent of whites said that they would vote for a well-qualified black presidential candidate and just 4 per cent approved of inter-racial marriages. By the end of the 1990s, the figures were 93 per cent and 61 per cent respectively.

Moreover, there is an emphasis on the degree to which the new minorities share traditional American cultural norms. Francis Fukuyama, author of *The End of History and the Last Man*, argues that many third-world immigrants are bound together by strong family structures, a faith in Roman Catholicism and a strong moral code (Fukuyama 1993: 28–9). There is also a widely shared commitment to the national language. About 90 per cent of Hispanics believe that anyone living in the US should learn English at the earliest opportunity (Leo 1997). In 1986 the public schools in Los Angeles turned away 40,000 adult immigrants because their English classes were full. There have, furthermore, been suggestions that although it traditionally took three generations for immigrant families to become fully fluent English speakers, the period has now been shortened to two generations.

In addition, most of those within the minority communities define themselves – first and foremost – as Americans. Although some have strong notions of group identity and significant numbers are not proud of particular events in American history, almost half the population go so far as to assert that being American is the 'most important thing in their life' (Citrin 2001: 296). Furthermore, a series of surveys conducted in Los Angeles and across the country during the 1990s suggested that clear majorities of blacks, Latinos and Asians thought of themselves as 'just an American' (Citrin 2001: 294).

Although those in the assimilationist camp accepts that there is growing religious diversity, they emphasise the degree to which many of these faiths, including Islam, can co-exist with each other and American cultural norms. About 70 per cent of black Muslims are associated with the American Muslim Mission rather than Louis Farrakhan's Nation of Islam. The Mission is led by Imam Warith Deen Muhammed and committed to the work ethic, family responsibilities, law enforcement and the American nation. The Imam himself has stated that 'America's great blessing is the freedom to acquire personal wealth, social mobility and move from city to city unhampered'. In the 1984 presidential election, he opposed Jesse Jackson, the radical black civil rights leader, and instead backed Ronald Reagan.

Between 1960 and 1990 there was an 800 per cent growth in the number of inter-racial marriages. A quarter of Hispanics marry non-Hispanics. A third of Asian-Americans are married to non-Asians. In total, one in twenty-five couples are inter-racial and more than three million children are of mixed race parentage. This has begun to change self-perceptions. In the 2000 Census 6.8 million defined themselves as multiracial. As Gary Gerstle notes, such people are 'often hailed as the harbingers of a new, less race conscious America' (Gerstle 2001). However, intermarriage levels are significantly lower for blacks, and some observers foresee the assimilation of Latinos and Asians as both seek to distance themselves from the black communities.

There are other indications that racism is losing its former potency. Although the South has traditionally been associated with the most overt expressions of prejudice, African-Americans are now 'returning' to the region in significant numbers. The metropolitan regions and suburbs of Florida and Georgia – most notably Atlanta – have been particularly attractive to black migrants. During the 1990s the black population in the South increased by 3,575,211. In contrast, there was a net out-migration of African-Americans from the Northeast, Midwest and West (Frey 2001b: 2).

The progress that minorities have made in terms of political representation should also not be neglected. For example, there has been a steady growth in the number of Latino office holders. The figure rose from 3,128 in 1984 to 5,191 in 1998 (*CQ Researcher* 1998a). Furthermore, there is evidence of a change of mood among minority representatives. A significant proportion are eschewing the politics of protest and are instead seeking 'colour-blind' solutions. The American political process has been **deracialised** in other ways. In *Shaw* v. *Reno* (1993) and subsequent rulings, the US Supreme Court struck down a 'majority-minority' district in North Carolina where the boundaries had been drawn – with bizarre geographical consequences – so as to ensure that minorities constituted an electoral majority. This led many observers to forecast a dramatic drop in minority representation in Congress. White voters, it was said, would not vote in sufficient numbers for minority candidates because racist sentiments were still too strong. However, such predictions were confounded. It seems that many whites are prepared to vote for black nominees, particularly incumbents. In both 1996 and 1998 black members of the House of Representatives were re-elected, despite the redrawing of boundaries in the wake of the Supreme Court ruling and the subsequent loss of black voters in the districts they represented. For example, in Georgia's second district – a rural, conservative area where the proportion of African-American voters was cut from 52 per cent to 35 per cent – Congressman Sanford Bishop won four out of every ten white votes.

Although the Republican Party lost support among Latinos and Asian-Americans during the 1990s, and some forms of voting have been divided along racial lines, this can be seen as an aberration rather than a fundamental realignment. Those who talk of assimilation point to the degree of consensus across the ethnic dividing lines and suggest that the adoption of more inclusive political strategies could win back those who have abandoned the party. They hope, for example, to see a greater number of minority candidates standing on the party's behalf. They cite the examples of J. C. Watts, a black Republican Congressman, and Matt Fong, an Asian-American who won the California 1998 Republican nomination for the US Senate. Furthermore, they observe, the Republican candidates who have actively sought out the minority vote have often been successful in gaining it. The re-election of George W. Bush to the governorship of Texas in November 1998 is widely cited as a model. He wooed the Latino communities, issued campaign advertisements in Spanish and, in contrast to the Republican Party's fortunes nationally, gained 49 per cent of the Latino vote (Walsh 1998: 23). Republican strategists believe that the party must follow this path if it is to win future presidential and congressional elections. As one adviser noted, the Latino vote is 'significant and growing' in 'all of the key states – California, Texas, Florida and New York' (quoted in Kirschten 1998: 54).

There are also claims that race has lost much of its former economic importance. William Julius Wilson of Harvard University – named by *Time* magazine as one of the twenty-five most influential Americans – refers to the 'declining significance of race'. Class has begun, he argues, to compete with race as the principal determinant of black life-chances (Wilson 1978). Race is no longer, therefore, the sole determinant of an individual's economic status. Although the black underclass has swelled since the 1960s, the black middle class has grown and, furthermore, prospered. Per capita real average annual income was 50 per cent greater in 1997 than it was in 1980. Average black household spending on new cars, clothes and personal computers outstrips white household spending.

Finally, despite the attention that some far Right organisations attract, incidents of racial violence are small in number. Between 1997 and 1999 only 2,976 'hate crimes' – those motivated by hatred for an individual's race, religion, sexual orientation, disability or national origin – were reported. During the same period, there were, in total, 5.4 million offences (*Washington Times* 2001).

Differences

The claims of both the Balkanisation and assimilationist camps should be subjected to scrutiny. The former often fails to distinguish between the different states and regions of the US. However, a contrast should be drawn between states and regions. There are, for example, differences between California and Texas. In California – for much of the 1990s – there was intense hostility towards both illegal and legal immigration. The cultural gulf between whites and the Latino communities was at its sharpest. The politics of the state were structured around the presence of the minority communities and the reactions of the white population. For example, Proposition 187 sought to ensure that illegal immigrants were refused non-essential state benefits and services, while

Proposition 209 brought affirmative action to an end in the provision of state services such as education. Former Republican Governor Pete Wilson backed these initiatives and also associated himself with calls for a constitutional amendment ending the right of children born in the US to automatic American citizenship.

Texas has, however, been different. As *The Economist* has noted, 'Texans have

---

Native Americans

In the late nineteenth century – following the military defeat of the native peoples, the seizure of land and the killing of the buffalo on which so many depended – US policy makers adopted a policy of forced assimilation. This continued for over half a century. In the 1950s, for example, Native Americans were encouraged to move to urban areas. Many of the reservations were taken over by the state authorities or the US Army.

From the 1960s onwards, however, there was a significant shift in both attitudes and policies. Mid-century liberalism laid the basis for a growing sense of guilt towards Native Americans. This stemmed partly from a growing awareness of the brutality – depicted in, for example, the 1970 film, *Soldier Blue* – to which the native people had been subjected in earlier years. It was also rooted in a growing commitment to ethnic pluralism. Cultural diversity, it was felt, should be celebrated. Earlier policies of enforced assimilation were increasingly seen as oppressive and authoritarian. There were, furthermore, feelings – at their most evident in *Dances with Wolves* (1990) – that native life had possessed a spiritual character from which more 'advanced' peoples could learn. Lastly, as attention turned during the 1960s to the poverty in the country's midst, the socio-economic position of Native Americans was brought into sharp relief. President Johnson described them as the 'forgotten Americans'. About 40 per cent were unemployed. Life expectancy was only 44 years (Gibson 1980: 558)

Against this background, protest organisations such as the National Indian Youth Conference were formed. In 1973, members of the American Indian Movement (AIM) occupied the village of Wounded Knee, South Dakota, where large numbers of Sioux families had been massacred in 1890. Government programmes – directed towards economic development, housing improvement and vocational training – were created. Heritage and cultural projects were funded. The Indian Civil Rights Act of 1968 provided an assurance that individual and group rights would be respected. The federal government also restored some tribes to trust status, laying the basis for assistance. There have, furthermore, been significant numbers of business ventures on the reservations. However, despite these measures, a 1990 study of the twenty-five largest tribes revealed significant disparities between Native Americans and the overall US population (US Census Bureau (1995).

crafted their quasi-nationalistic identity, at least in part, in relation to Mexico. Texan cities have imbibed Mexican culture . . . Latino hybrids, such as Tex-Mex cuisine and Tejano music, are common currency' (*The Economist* 1996). Although these descriptions of cultural fusion are only partially representative and many Texan cities are marked by residential segregation, the differences between California and Texas remain. Furthermore, they have significant political consequences. The issues that have defined California Republicanism can be contrasted with Texas Republican Governor George W. Bush's emphasis on 'compassionate conservatism'. Whereas California's electorate passed Proposition 209, the voters of Houston rejected attempts to end affirmative action programmes by a 45 per cent margin in November 1997.

The arguments associated with the assimilationist perspective should also be subjected to scrutiny. First, the concept of assimilationism is itself problematic. It has cultural, economic and political dimensions that must be disentangled. Structural assimilation – by which a minority establishes friendships and other personal ties with other groupings – should be distinguished from acculturation. The Asian-American communities are associated with a commitment to 'American' values such as entrepreneurship and the work ethic, but they remain otherwise culturally distinct. Second, as developments in Texas suggest, some hybrid cultures are emerging.

Lastly, alongside these arguments, there appears to be a process of **segmented assimilation**. The US no longer has widely shared and accepted cultural norms. The certainties about American national identity – which marked out earlier generations and led to a high level of consensus around social and cultural values – have given way to a plethora of contending identities. Contemporary immigrants are being drawn towards different cultures and lifestyles, both functional and dysfunctional:

> In the absence of a relatively uniform 'mainstream' whose mores and prejudices dictate a common path of integration, we observe today several distinct forms of adaptation. One of them replicates the time-honored portrayal of growing acculturation and parallel integration into the white middle-class; a second leads straight in the opposite direction to permanent poverty and assimilation to the underclass; still a third combines rapid economic advancement with deliberate preservation of the immigrant community's values and solidarity. (Portes and Zhou 1994)

Summary

Shifting demographic patterns have led some to talk of Balkanisation. They represent the US as a divided society, emphasising residential segregation and attitudinal differences. They also assert that the mechanisms that traditionally assimilated newcomers have been undermined by policy shifts since the 1960s.

Others – particularly multiculturalists and some large-scale business interests – also see the US as a segmented society, but talk in terms of embracing diversity. All these arguments have, however, been countered by those who stress the degree to which there are shared values and interests across all demographic groupings. However, there are significant differences between regions and states.

References and further reading

Alba R. and V. Nee (1997) , 'Rethinking assimilation theory for a new era of immigration', *International Migration Review*, 31:4, Winter, 826–74

Alsop, R. J. (ed.)(1998), *The Wall Street Journal Almanac 1999*, New York, Ballantine Books.

Amiri Baraka, A. (1998), 'Multinational, multicultural America versus white supremacy', in I. Reed (ed.), *MultiAmerica: Essays on Cultural Wars and Cultural Peace*, New York, Penguin Books, 391–4.

Ashbee, E. (2000), 'America divided: the politics of "Balkanization"', in A. Grant (ed.), *American Politics: 2000 and Beyond*, Aldershot, Aldgate, 7–27.

Berube, M. (1997), 'Past imperfect, present tense', *The Nation*, 12 May, www.thenation.com/issue/9/05120512beru.htm

Brimelow, P. (1996), *Alien Nation*, New York, HarperPerennial.

Brimelow, P. and E. Rubenstein (1997), 'Electing a new people', *National Review*, 16 June, 32–4.

Campbell, E. D. C. and K. S. Rice (1991), *Before Freedom Came: African-American Life in the Antebellum South*, Richmond/Charlottesville, Museum of the Confederacy/University Press of Virginia.

Campo-Flores, A. (2000), 'Brown against brown', *Newsweek*, 18 September, 49.

Citrin, J. (2001), 'The end of American identity?' in S.A. Renshon (ed.), *One America? Political Leadership, National Identity, and the Dilemmas of Diversity*, Washington DC, Georgetown University Press, 285–307.

Cohn, D. (2001), 'New census information reveals larger than expected number of illegal immigrants', *The Washington Post*, 25 October.

CQ Researcher (1998a), 23 January.

CQ Researcher (1998b), 18 September.

Custred, G. (1997), 'Country time', *National Review*, 16 June.

De la Garza, R. O, A. Falcon, F. C. Garcia and J. Garcia (1994), 'Mexican immigrants, Mexican Americans, and American political culture', in B. Edmonston and J. S. Passel (eds), *Immigration and Ethnicity*, Washington DC, Urban Institute Press, 227–51.

The Economist (1996), 13 July.

The Economist (1997), 15 February.

Ellis, M. and R. Wright (1998), 'The Balkanization metaphor in the analysis of US immigration', *Annals of the Association of American Geographers*, 88:4, 686–98.

Fields, R. (2001), 'Demographics: experts clash over the degree of black assimilation', *Los Angeles Times*, 24 June.

Fields, R. and R. Herndon (2001), 'Segregation of a new sort takes shape', *Los Angeles Times*, 5 July.

Frazier, E. F. (1965), *Black Bourgeoisie*, New York, The Free Press.

Frey, W. H. (1996), 'Immigration, domestic migration, and democratic Balkanization in America: new evidence for the 1990s', *Population and Development Review*, 22:4, December, 741–63.

Frey, W. H. (1999), 'Melting pot moves to the suburbs', *Newsday*, 4 August, A37.

Frey, W. H. (2001a), 'A close look at the melting pot myth', *Newsday*, 19 March, A23.

Frey, W. H. (2001b), *Census 2000 Shows Large Black Return to the South, Reinforcing the Region's "White-Black" Demographic Profile*, Ann Arbor, University of Michigan – Population Studies Center at the Institute for Social Research, PSC Research Report 01–473.

Fukuyama, F. (1993), 'Immigrants and family values', *Commentary*, 95:5, May, 26–32.

Gerstle, G. (2001), 'Making sense of the new census', *San Francisco Chronicle*, 11 July, A 17.

Gibson, A. M. (1980), *The American Indian: Prehistory to Present*, Lexington, D. C. Heath.

Glazer, N. and D. P. Moynihan (1967), *Beyond the Melting Pot: The Negroes, Puerto Ricans, Jews, Italians and Irish of New York City*, Cambridge, The MIT Press.

Gleason, P. (1982), 'American identity and Americanization', in W. Petersen, M. Novak and P. Gleason (eds), *Concepts of Ethnicity*, Cambridge, MA, The Belknap Press of Harvard University Press, 57–143.

Guinier, L. (1994), *The Tyranny of the Majority: Fundamental Fairness in Representative Democracy*, New York, The Free Press.

Hajnal Z. and M. Baldassare (2001), *Finding Common Ground: Racial and Ethnic Attitudes in California*, San Francisco, Public Policy Institute of California.

Hochschild, J. (1995), *Facing Up to the American Dream: Race, Class, and the Soul of the Nation*, Princeton: Princeton University Press.

Huntington, S. P. (1997), 'American identity: the erosion of American national interests', *Current*, November, 8–16.

Institutional Investor (1995), August.

Jacoby, T. (1998), *Someone Else's House: America's Unfinished Struggle for Integration*, New York, The Free Press.

Johnson, G. (2001), 'Gaining insight into the Latino middle class', *Los Angeles Times*, 11 June.

Kazal, R. A. (1995), 'Revisiting assimilation: the rise, fall, and reappraisal of a concept in American ethnic history', *American Historical Review*, 100:2, April, 437–71.

Kerber, L. K. (1989), 'Diversity and transformation of American studies', *American Quarterly*, 41:3, September, 415–31.

Kirschten, D. (1998), 'Trying a little tenderness', *National Journal*, 10 January, 54.

Kitano, H. H. L. (1980), 'Japanese', in S. Thernstrom (ed.), *Harvard Encyclopedia of American Ethnic Groups*, Cambridge, The Belknap Press of Harvard University Press, 561–71.

Lai, H. M. (1980), 'Chinese', in S. Thernstrom (ed.), *Harvard Encyclopedia of American Ethnic Groups*, Cambridge, MA, The Belknap Press of Harvard University Press, 217–34.

Leo, J. (1997), 'A dubious "diversity" report', *US News and World Report*, 23 June, www.usnews.com/usnews/issue/970623/23john.htm

Marable, M. (1985), *Black American Politics: From the Washington Marches to Jesse Jackson*, London, Verso.

Melendy, H. B. (1980), 'Filipinos', in S. Thernstrom (ed.), *Harvard Encyclopedia of American Ethnic Groups*, Cambridge, MA, The Belknap Press of Harvard University Press, 354–62.

Morone, J. A. (1996), 'The struggle for American culture', *PS: Political Science and Politics*, 28:3, September, 424–30.

Nelson, B. A. (1994), *America Balkanized: immigration's challenge to government*, Monterey, The American Immigration Control Foundation.

Novak, M. (1972), *The Rise of the Unmeltable Ethnics; Politics and Culture in the Seventies*, New York, Macmillan.

Portes, A. and M. Zhou (1994), 'Should immigrants assimilate?', *Public Interest*, 116, Summer, heather.cs.ucdavis.edu/pub/Immigration/Portes.html

Renshon, S. A. (2001), 'America at a crossroads: political leadership, national identity, and the decline of common culture', in S.A. Renshon (ed.), *One America? Political Leadership, National Identity, and the Dilemmas of Diversity*, Washington DC, Georgetown University Press, 3–27.

Roy, D. L. (1999), *Summary Results from the Latino Ethnic Attitude Survey*, Lawrence, University of Kansas, falcon.cc.ukans.edu/~droy

Schlesinger, A. M. Jr (1992), *The Disuniting of America*, New York, W. W. Norton.

Schmitt, E. (2001), 'Census figures show Hispanics pulling even with blacks', *The New York Times*, 8 March.

Schwarz, B. (1995), 'The diversity myth: America's leading export', *The Atlantic Monthly*, May.

Smith, T. W. and L. Jarkko (1998), *National Pride: A Cross-National Analysis*, GSS Cross-National Report 19, Chicago, University of Chicago – National Opinion Research Center.

Thernstrom S. and A. Thernstrom (1997), *America in Black and White: One Nation, Indivisible*, New York, Simon & Schuster.

Trueba, E. H. T. (1999), *Latinos Unidos: From Cultural Diversity to the Politics of Solidarity*, Lanham, Rowman & Littlefield.

USA Today (2001), 'Draft registration rises', 5 May.

US Census Bureau (1993), *We the American . . . Hispanics*, Washington DC, US Department of Commerce.

US Census Bureau (1995), *Selected Social and Economic Characteristics for the 25 largest American Indian Tribes, 1990* www.census.gov/population/socdemo/race/indian/ailangz.txt.

US Census Bureau (2001), *Census 2000 Supplementary Survey Summary Tables – Profile of Selected Social Characteristics*, factfinder.census.gov/servlet/ QTTable?ds_name=ACS_C2SS_EST_G00_&geo_id=01000US&qr_name=ACS_C2SS_EST_G00_QT02.

Walsh, K. T. (1998), 'Can he save the Republicans?', *US News and World Report*, 16 November.

Walzer, M. (1996), *What It Means To Be An American*, New York, Marsilio.

Washington Times (2001), 1 October

Wickham, D. (2001), 'Root out black murderers', *USA Today*, 4 December.

Wilson, W. J. (1978), *The Declining Significance of Race: Blacks and Changing American Institutions*, Chicago, University of Chicago Press.

Wilson, W. J. (1987), *The Truly Disadvantaged: The Inner City, the Underclass, and Public Policy*, Chicago, The University of California Press.

Williamson C. Jr (n.d.), 'Promises to keep', in The Rockford Institute, *Immigration and the*

American Identity: Selections from Chronicles: A Magazine of American Culture, 1985–1995, Rockford, The Rockford Institute.

Wolfe, A. (1996), 'Affirmative action inc.', *The New Yorker*, November 25.

Wright, J. W. (2001), *The New York Times Almanac 2001*, New York, Penguin.

Zia, H. (2000), *Asian American Dreams: The Emergence of an American People*, New York, Farrar, Straus & Giroux.

7

One nation indivisible: the American regions

As Eric Hobsbawm records, the concept of American nationhood was not fully embraced until long after the formation of the US: 'Early political discourse in the USA preferred to speak of "the people", "the union", "the confederation", "our common land", "the public", "public welfare", or "the community" in order to avoid the centralizing and unitary implications of the term "nation" against the rights of the federated states' (Hobsbawm 1999: 18).

However, patriotic sentiments grew during the nineteenth and twentieth centuries and were reflected in the progressive adoption of formal national symbols, such as an agreed flag, memorials and the national anthem (Krakau 1997: 10). Generations of American schoolchildren were taught to begin the day by reciting the Pledge of Allegiance and affirming their commitment to 'one nation, indivisible, with liberty and justice for all'. The words 'under God' were later added. Others used the American's Creed. This was a declaration of faith in American democracy and an injunction 'to support its Constitution; to obey its laws; to respect its flag; and to defend it against all enemies' (*Washington Times* 2001). The shift towards a sense of national purpose and nationhood was a consequence of a number of events and processes.

First, the Civil War (1861–5) established that the US was one country rather than a mere association of separate and quasi-sovereign states. Significantly, observers spoke of the US in plural terms ('they') before the war and in the singular afterwards. As industrialisation progressed, corporations carved out a national, unified market for their products. Particular brands became household names. The identical character of the products and services that were sold across the nation created a sense of homogeneity. Market processes thereby broke down the barriers between disparate and largely insular communities.

During the Progressive era in the years preceding the First World War (1917–18), ideas of a more centralised nation and an activist national government, expressed in, for example, Herbert Croly's book, *The Promise of American Life*, won increasing acceptance (Croly 1989). The national government continued to grow in importance as the twentieth century progressed, particularly during the New Deal and Great Society years of the 1930s and 1960s. Feelings of patriotism were also intensified by Americanisation campaigns. During the opening decades of the twentieth century, government authorities and voluntary organisations worked together to teach English, promote national loyalty and encourage assimilation among immigrants.

Although some foreign conflicts – particularly Vietnam – divided the country, most wars and periods of international tension brought citizens together in a sense of shared purpose. Later film representations of army units in the Second World War (1939–45) emphasise this. Many – including Stephen Spielberg's *Saving Private Ryan* – have typically included individuals drawn from a diversity of ethnic and regional backgrounds who come together against a common foe. The attacks on the World Trade Center and the Pentagon in September 2001 appear to have similarly galvanised and united American citizens, although was some evidence of hostility towards Arab-Americans.

While American culture has always emphasised the virtues of movement, the construction of the railroads and the growth of air travel facilitated greater geographical mobility over longer distances. Other developments encouraged individuals to take advantage of this. For example, the retirement pension reduced the dependence of older citizens upon their families and allowed them to settle in states such as Florida. Moreover, although many television networks and newspapers are still locally or state based, many of their features are syndicated or are drawn from the national networks. The film and music industries are based upon a national market. This has led to the increasing 'nationalisation' of US popular culture.

The growth of the city – or 'megalopolis' – and the subsequent evolution of the surrounding metropolitan region also increased geographical mobility, undermined the traditional boundaries between regions and cut across state lines. The New York metropolitan region, for example, encompasses parts of New York state, New Jersey and Connecticut. During the latter half of the twentieth century there were further shifts. Suburbanisation drew many of those who were in secure employment away from the central cities. New highways allowed many to commute over greater distances and rural areas were increasingly tied to the cities and suburbs, creating 'rurban' belts. While in 1940 the city held 75 per cent of the New York metropolitan region's population, the figure had fallen to 40 per cent by 1980. In the closing years of the twentieth century, there was, as Chapter 6 recorded, an exodus from the largest multi-ethnic metropolitan regions to the predominantly white heartlands.

Difference and distinctiveness

The extent to which the US is centralised can, however, be exaggerated. Each of the fifty states has a separate history, system of law and structure of government. Some have a distinctive cultural character. Utah is, for example, closely associated with the Mormon faith (Elazar 1994: 277). Furthermore, as Daniel Elazar emphasises, even states that at first sight appear to possess few defining features have particular characteristics:

> Every state has its own particular identity, matched by the realities of its distinctiveness . . . a moment's reflection does bring something special to mind. And behind that 'something special' there is a reality forged by history, geography, and culture and embodied in particular patterns of political organization focusing on a particular conception of justice. (Elazar 1994: 279)

Regions

Alongside the states, there are also discernible regions. This concept, however, requires definition. Traditionally, it was defined as 'a tract of land with relatively homogeneous characteristics and marked boundaries', and commonly used to describe particular clusters of states (Bradshaw 1988: 7). Furthermore, there were familiar regional images and stereotypes:

> There is the Yankee from New England with commerce as their main interest and a rather clipped accent. There is the easy-going southern white speaking in a singsong drawl. There is the dour mid-westerner with limited, small-town horizons. There is the boasting Texan with the ten-gallon hat, and there is the way-out Californian, forging ahead into new fields hardly imagined by others. (Bradshaw 1988: 9)

The concept of the 'region' is not, however, straightforward. It is an artificial **construct** imposed by those studying the subject (Faragher 1999). Some surveys stress the physical features of an area and refer, for example, to the Rocky mountains or the Appalachians as distinct regions. Most observers suggest, however, that regions are formed from the economic and cultural differences between areas (Gastil 1975: 25).

What is the basis of these differences? The 'doctrine of first effective settlement' has provided an influential answer. This suggests that the regions were shaped and structured by the folkways of the first European colonists. In his 1991 book, *Albion's Seed,* David Hackett Fischer argues that the US can be understood in terms of four regions, each of which had – and still has – distinctive **folkways**. By folkways, Fischer is describing the patterns of everyday life and traditions that shape individuals and communities. These include, for example, styles of speech as well as attitudes towards the family, child rearing, education, religious customs, work, government and the acquisition of wealth. The different American folkways, Fischer asserts, were brought to the American continent during the seventeenth century by settlers who came from distinct areas in the British Isles.

In the Massachusetts region, other Puritan families followed in the wake of the first Pilgrims, many making the journey during the 1630s. Fischer points out that they were disproportionately drawn from the eastern counties of England, most notably Suffolk, Essex and Norfolk, and they brought the folkways of these areas to this part of the New World. The origins of the early communities in Virginia in the decades after the founding of the Jamestown settlement were markedly different. The colonists were drawn largely from the South and West of England. During the 1650s many of the 'distressed cavaliers' and Royalists who had backed Charles I in the English Civil War (1642–9) sought refuge from the Cromwellian Commonwealth. They were to be followed by those who held much lower social ranks. More than 75 per cent were indentured servants – single males who, in return for payment of their passage across the Atlantic, were bound to work for a master over a given number of years. In contrast with Massachusetts and New England, Virginia was associated with the Church of England. Indeed, in 1642, the Governor required nonconformists to leave the colony.

A majority of the 23,000 who settled in the Delaware Valley between 1675 and 1725 were Quakers. They came from the Midlands and northern counties of England – including Derbyshire, Nottinghamshire, Lancashire and Yorkshire – and left a cultural imprint on states such as Pennsylvania. Many were farmers and tradesman of middling rank who sought sanctuary from religious persecution in England and spiritual freedom in the New World. In contrast with Puritanism, they saw God in benevolent terms. Their communities were closely knit and regulated almost every aspect of life. Although English Quakers had become a minority as early as 1760, they remained a dominant grouping for long afterwards.

During the eighteenth century – particularly between 1717 and 1775 – the first settlers were followed by migrants from Scotland, the north of Ireland and northern England. They generally had more humble social origins than those who preceded them, although few were from the poorest rungs of British society. However, they came as free men and women rather than indentured servants. After landing at American ports such as Philadelphia, they settled on the outer edges of the area that had been settled by European colonists. It was dangerous territory. As Fischer records: 'Many drifted south and west along the mountains of Maryland, Virginia and the Carolinas. They gradually became the dominant English-speaking culture in a broad belt of territory that extended from the highlands of Appalachia through much of the Old Southwest' (Fischer 1991: 633–4). Although many were Presbyterians or low-church Anglicans, the 'backcountry' settlers sought personal betterment. They had an individualist spirit and resented the imposition of formal authority. There was a border culture in which disputes were, more often that not, resolved by violence or summary justice.

There were, then, significant cultural differences between the regions. Each, for example, had its own conception of liberty. In New England there was an emphasis upon the freedom of communities to worship God but, at the same time, little dissent within the communities themselves was permitted. In Virginia, liberty was defined in terms of the right of established elites to be left alone and maintain their rule over others. In contrast, the Quakers of the Delaware Valley had much more egalitarian and individualist notions of freedom and they were to be among the first to oppose slavery. Lastly, in the southern backcountry, there was an emphasis upon individuals' rights to protect themselves and their family.

Towards the end of the eighteenth century, the calls for revolution and independence arose when these different notions of liberty were challenged by a fifth cultural formation. In Britain, a new elite emerged following the final crushing of the threat posed by Jacobite rebels in 1745. It sought political and cultural change, both within Britain and in the colonies. This demanded the suppression of traditional rights and liberties. As Fischer records: 'The people of the four regions had long enjoyed their distinguishable liberties, many of them for nearly two centuries. A common enemy made for a common cause' (Fischer 1991: 73). Fischer argues that, as the nineteenth century progressed, later generations of immigrants were absorbed into the four established cultural traditions. At the same time, the geographical territory occupied by these distinct cultures spread so as to incorporate much of the US. The folkways of the seventeenth and eighteenth centuries thereby moulded the cultural character of contemporary America.

Fischer suggests that the dialects to be found in New England today have their origins in eastern England. Similarly, homicide rates, levels of educational achievement, attitudes regarding the role of women and opinion towards both government and education all have a regional character and owe their origins to the folkways of the first settlers. Patterns of voting behaviour and political attitudes also conform to these regional patterns. During the 1980s support for the campaign to halt the construction of further nuclear weapons and responses to a number of other issues were structured, he argues, on the basis of regions that had taken shape in the seventeenth century: 'The nuclear freeze, for example, was supported by all but a few New England Congressmen, and opposed by most Representatives from the south and west. In attitudes towards military affairs, foreign policy, capital punishment and many domestic questions, regional attitudes are still powerful' (Fischer 1991: 885).

When an attempt was made to codify women's equality through the proposed Equal Rights Amendment to the US Constitution, every northern state voted in favour. Conversely, the measure was opposed by the southern states. Fischer also notes that the widely shared opposition to gun control in the South and West was shaped by 'the retributive and every-man-his-own-master principles of the border legacy' (Fischer 1991: 73). At the same time, the institutions of local government also continue to reproduce the different attitudes bequeathed by early colonists. In New England, and in the northern tier of states that were later settled by those from New England, there are town meetings allowing a measure of local self-government. In Virginia and the coastal South, however, more hierarchical traditions have been maintained and decision making is concentrated in the 'county courthouse elites' (Fischer 1991: 895).

Daniel Elazar (1994) approaches the formation of regions in a similar way, although he employs a different typology. He argues that there were three original American 'sections' – New England, the middle states and the South – and each had a distinct cultural character. The Puritan vision upon which Yankee New England built itself was moralistic. There was a commitment to a commonwealth based upon shared principles. In contrast, those living in the middle states were more individualistic. They sought a society that permitted the pursuit of private ends. Against this background, the political order was perceived as a marketplace within which citizens engaged in bargaining so as to reconcile their conflicting wants. The South was, however, ambivalent about notions such as these. Instead, there was a traditionalist emphasis upon order and hierarchy.

During the eighteenth and nineteenth centuries, each of these original sections expanded westward (Elazar 1994: 26). As they did so, some of the cultural characteristics of each were reproduced in the areas that were settled. These migratory patterns have continued to this day: 'Southerners continue to flow into areas settled by southerners and even expand into contiguous ones; Yankees follow old migration lines established by their forebears' (Elazar 1994: 219). As a consequence, Elazar suggests, seventeen states in the North and Northwest have a predominantly moralistic culture, sixteen in the 'greater South' have a traditionalist culture, and a further seventeen – stretching across the middle in a southwesterly direction – are individualistic in character (Elazar 1994: 282–85).

Studies of the regions that rest upon the ties between the first settlers and contemporary cultural formations are, however, open to criticism. Some critics of *Albion's Seed* argue that the periods of migration during the seventeenth and early eighteenth centuries had a looser and less monolithic character than the book suggests. Indeed, Fischer concedes that only three-fifths of New Englanders came from East Anglia. The early settlements therefore probably had much less cultural cohesion and fewer well-defined folkways than it initially appears.

Moreover, from the earliest days, there were encounters between colonists and Native Americans. These – together with life on the edges between 'civilisation' and the 'wilderness' – reshaped attitudes and expectations. It was here, Frederick Jackson Turner asserted in 1893, that the American character was forged (see Chapter 1). Fischer also pays relatively little attention to the role of African-Americans in shaping American identity. The first blacks were brought to Virginia as indentured servants in 1619. Despite slavery and institutional forms of oppression, they played a part in shaping American cultural forms, particularly the South.

Furthermore, later colonists and immigrants were not simply absorbed into the established cultural traditions. As other chapters have recorded, there was large-scale immigration from countries apart from the British Isles. Indeed, only 19 per cent of those in the US today have British ancestry (see Chapter 6). Some regions owe their historical development and character to these immigrants. From the late eighteenth century onwards, German settlers in Pennsylvania, Maryland and Virginia began moving westward towards the Northwest Territory that was opened up in 1787. Seventy-five years later, the 1862 Homestead Act offered 160 acres to immigrants who agreed to farm the land for at least five years and pledged to take US citizenship. A process of chain migration brought further German-American friends and family to the Midwest (Heinrich 2001). Indeed, although many came to adopt multiple forms of identity, some of the communities from other European countries maintained their languages and civic organisations until the First World War. As Elazar acknowledges: 'The settlement and migration of these groups can be viewed as laid on top of, fitted to, and affected by the bedrock of the three broader subcultures' (Elazar 1994: 217).

At the same time, although the concept of the 'melting pot' should be regarded with caution, the cultural character of cities such as New York, Chicago and San Francisco was also remade by waves of immigration during the nineteenth and twentieth centuries, (see Chapter 1). Similarly, the western US has a distinct cultural character that cannot be represented as the simple imposition of eastern folkways that had their origins in the British Isles. Settlement was a social process resting on an interaction between individuals, communities and the environment. California was, for example, shaped by its identification with opportunity, its climate, the Pacific Ocean and Asian immigration.

It is therefore legitimate to think in terms of other regions apart from those formed by the first colonists and subsequent migratory patterns that grew outwards from them. Some observers talk of between six and sixteen regions, including the South, New England, the Midwest and West.

The South

Despite disagreement about its borders, most observers talk of the South as a distinct and separate region. Indeed, some have talked of 'southern exceptionalism'. Up until the 1960s, the southern identity appeared to rest largely upon a historical legacy that marked it out from the remainder of the country. While the northern states had ended slavery by the mid-nineteenth century, the slave system was integral to the South's agrarian economy. Fearing northern domination, and the abolition of slavery, the South broke away from the US in 1861 and established itself as a separate country: the Confederate States of America or **Confederacy**. Southern secession provoked the Civil War that culminated,

---

Defining the 'South'

The difficulties in identifying and demarcating the American regions are particularly evident in studies of the South. It has been subject to different definitions:

- Some think of the South as the eleven states that broke away from the US in 1860–61 and formed the Confederacy.
- Others represent the South as the slave-owning states that lay below the Mason–Dixon line, which was drawn between 1763 and 1768 to establish the boundaries of Pennsylvania and Maryland. Some of these were slave states, but remained loyal to the US during the Civil War.
- However, *Congressional Quarterly*, and polling organisations such as the Gallup Organization include only thirteen states (Stanley and Niemi 2000: 406–7).

---

after four years, in northern victory. The defeat of the Confederacy enabled the US to remain united as one country.

While slavery was abolished following passage of the Thirteenth Amendment at the end of the Civil War, circumstances compelled most African-Americans to work as **sharecroppers**. They tended the small, often uneconomic, plots of land that were leased to them. However, the landowners took a large proportion of the crops that were gathered. Furthermore, many sharecroppers had to borrow so as to buy seeds, fertilisers and provisions, and were – as a consequence – condemned to remain in debt. Blacks also faced other forms of oppression. From the 1890s onwards, the Jim Crow laws (see page 101) led to the imposition of segregation across the southern states. Blacks were confined to separate and unequal facilities. Notions of white racial supremacy also gave birth to organisations such as the Ku-Klux-Klan. There were an estimated 4,753 lynchings between 1882 and 1968. Many were public spectacles and nearly all the victims were African-Americans. Although the number of lynchings fell as the twentieth century progressed, institutionalised – or *de jure* – discrimination only came to a close when the 1964 Civil Rights Act – which outlawed segregation – and the 1965 Voting Rights Act – which ensured that African-Americans could freely participate in elections – were passed. By the mid-1990s, schools in the former Confederacy were more racially mixed than those in Northeast, Midwest and West (Stanley and Niemi 2000: 374–5).

Southern distinctiveness does not, however, rest upon race or memories of the Civil War alone. Indeed, in the years since the demise of segregation, southern identity has opened itself out to blacks as well as whites. As John Shelton Reed observes: 'These days southern identification is not so much a matter of shared history as a shared cultural style – some cultural conservatism, religiosity, manners, speech, humor, music, that sort of thing' (Fox-Genovese and Genovese 2001)

Some of the region's critics have represented this cultural style in terms of anti-modernism and backwardness. However, there have been, and continue to be those who represent the southern legacy in more positive terms. In particular, there are suggestions that the region's conservative traditions convey 'much of intrinsic value that will have to be incorporated in the world view of any political movement . . . that expects to arrest our plunge into moral decadence and national decline' (Genovese 1996: 7). In the 1930s the Agrarians – a group based at Vanderbilt University – denounced the anonymity and competitiveness of city culture and celebrated the stable, organic character of southern society. Eugene Genovese has echoed this. He argues that southern conservatism held out against industrialisation and resisted the imposition of crude market values in which all relationships were reduced to financial transactions or a crude *cash nexus*. Instead of this, he asserts, southern identity rested upon community, order and reciprocity. There were firmly rooted notions of right and wrong.

It is widely accepted that the South progressively lost its distinct character during the course of the twentieth century. Those who talk in these terms argue that many southerners were 'Americanised' through service in the US army during the Spanish-American War of 1898. They also point to the absorption of southern commerce into a nationally structured market, the increasingly national character of American economic life and the changing nature of many southern cities. Atlanta has, for example, attracted large numbers of migrants from other parts of the US. John Samuel Ezell concludes that: 'By 1975 few areas of Southern life could be said to be distinctively different from the North. Those which could be pointed out were usually mental and emotional, long-established traditions from the past' (Ezell 1988: 476).

Another approach points to the decline of southern distinctiveness, but depicts it in different terms. It suggests that southern politics, religious beliefs, culture and music have all progressively been accepted by other Americans. In particular, from the 1960s onwards, southern conservatism played a part in remaking the Republicans as an overtly right-wing party. From this perspective, there has been a 'southernisation' of America.

However, despite shifts and changes, others maintain that the South has still retained a distinct identity that marks it out from the remainder of the US. For example, although promises of a 'new south' began to be fulfilled from the 1960s onwards and southern cities – most notably Atlanta – attracted inward investment and experienced high levels of growth, the South remains the poorest of the regions. In 2000 the median household income level was $38,410 compared with $42,148 for the US as a whole (US Census Bureau 2001). Moreover, the labour unions have traditionally been weaker in the south and there are also greater levels of hostility towards union activity. In addition, crime rates are significantly higher in the South. At the same time, the law is enforced with greater severity. The death penalty is, for example, more widely applied.

Although the differences are not dramatic, there are also higher levels of religious commitment in the South. As Table 7.1 indicates, many are evangelical 'born-again' Christians, for whom conversion was a profound personal experience. Their beliefs take a conservative form and significant numbers understand the Bible as a literal account of human history. There is also widespread backing for the reintroduction of school prayer and opposition to abortion (Escott and Goldfield 1990: 653).

Table 7.1   *Born-again Christians, 1988–98*

Reborn	South	Rest of US
Yes	50.2%	29.7%
No	49.8%	70.3%
N	1,459	2,750

Note: The South in this survey is based upon the definitions used by the US Census Bureau. The surveys were conducted in 1988–91 and 1998.
Source: Adapted from General Social Survey, 2001.

The conservatism of the south has had political consequences. It laid much of the basis for the evolution and growth of the Christian Right, which had a significant national presence during the 1980s and 1990s. It has also shaped voting patterns. From the late nineteenth century onwards – when the vote was largely confined to whites – the region was a Democratic Party stronghold. In 1952, for example, 83 per cent of southerners were Democrats (Glaser 1996: 7). For this reason, the region was known as the 'solid South'. However, the growing association between the Democratic Party and the civil rights movement led to **realignment**. Although African-Americans gained the right to vote and became the Democrats' most loyal constituency, whites increasingly shifted their loyalties – at least in presidential elections – towards the Republicans. Some argue that they were drawn to Republican candidates because of their opposition to welfare dependency and commitment to law enforcement. These themes, it has been said, are 'racially coded' and rest on a subliminal appeal to racist sentiments.

New England

The early character of New England – the six northeastern states – was charted in Chapter 1. Although not all of the initial settlers were Puritans, Puritanism shaped the culture of the region and shaped the basis of 'Yankee' identity.

Furthermore, the boundaries of belief were tightly circumscribed. There was an emphasis upon 'organic unity', as David Hackett Fischer (1991) calls it, rather than individual liberty. Those – such as Anne Hutchinson – who dissented from the established articles of faith were banished. The witchcraft trials that were held in Salem at the end of the seventeenth century can be understood as a form of social control.

There was, however, a progressive shift away from the initial goals of the first settlers – or **declension**. Although Puritan thinking emphasised hard work and the spirit of capitalism, it also subordinated individual interests to the collective will of the community. However, as trade and commerce began to spread, the individualist and competitive values associated with a market economy took root: 'At different rates in different places, the ideal of the collective good began to yield inexorably to the pull of individual interest as social cohesion became strained from various quarters and the opportunity for profit in trade increased' (Williams 1993).

Furthermore, although there were relatively few immigrants from other countries and backgrounds, Jewish communities were established in cities such as Boston and Providence. At the time of the War of Independence (1775–83), about 5 per cent of the New England population was not of English birth or descent. From the 1830s onwards, large numbers of Irish migrants settled in New England, most notably in Boston. For decades they attracted hostility. Their Catholicism appeared clannish and to represent allegiance to a foreign authority. Many were unskilled and illiterate, and seemed ready to work for low wages. During the First Great Awakening, other faiths such as the Baptists also began to challenge the hegemony of Puritan Congregationalism.

Against this background, and in the aftermath of the revolutionary war, entrepreneurs established the textile industry along the New England rivers such as the Merrimack. Mill towns – such as Lowell – were built, drawing in labourers from Canada and newly arrived immigrants from Europe. By 1908 workers with Yankee parents made up less than 10 per cent of the workforce in the Lowell mills (National Park Service 1992: 68). However, the Depression of the 1930s led to widespread closures, and the growing importance of commerce and finance and industry in other regions led to the economic eclipse of New England.

In the latter half of the twentieth century, however, there were the beginnings of a shift. The growth of high-tech electronic industries in the 1980s contributed to the 'Massachusetts miracle'. There was a process of urban renewal in cities such as Boston and New Haven. Interstate highways opened up the more remote corners of the region. Significant numbers from the northeastern cities bought second homes. For others, it offered retirement possibilities. There was also a process of 'overspill' from Massachusetts. Furthermore, alongside long-established and nationally pre-eminent universities such as Harvard and Yale, there was a burgeoning education 'industry'. In 1990, 239 colleges and universities were located in the region, 120 of which were in Massachusetts.

Tourism blossomed around the coast, ski resorts and at recreations of the region's historical past. Some companies were built, and products marketed, around New England's associations with nostalgia, practicality and the outdoor life.

The Midwest

Although definitions are problematic, the Midwest refers to the twelve states that divide the eastern seaboard states from the Rocky mountains. These include Illinois, Michigan, Minnesota and Iowa. Much of the region was only settled after the War of Independence. Some migrants made the journey from New England. However, in the latter half of the nineteenth century the Midwest also attracted immigrants. By 1880 the foreign-born comprised 23.7 per cent of the population in Michigan, 30.8 per cent in Wisconsin and 34.4 per cent in Minnesota. A large proportion was drawn from Germany and Scandinavia (Gray 1993).

The opening up of the West transformed the character of Chicago. It became a railway hub and staging post. Wood and goods for the homesteaders went westwards, while wheat, corn, cattle, and hogs went east. Mail order companies that were based in the city flourished. Other Midwest cities took off at a later stage. Detroit was built around the automobile industry, in particular Ford's Model T, which made the car accessible to a mass market. The city grew from a quarter million in 1900 to over one-and-a-half million by 1930.

In the latter half of the twentieth century, racial unrest and the decline of the traditional industrial sector – in the wake of recession and foreign competition – led to decay and very low levels of population growth. Michigan gained just 0.7 per cent during the 1980s. The pollution of the Great Lakes added to the sense of decline. There is still, however, a sense of regional identity that has been built upon the beginnings of recovery. After a clean-up operation, pollution levels in Lake Erie were substantially reduced. Following rationalisation, heavy industry has become more competitive and, in some areas, new industries have been established. The region still has an agricultural base, which continues to provide prosperity for those who survived the farm crisis of the mid-1980s.

The West

The West, particularly California, has long been associated – at least in mainstream American thought – with notions of opportunity. Indeed, it has mythic significance and some have spoken of the Californian 'dream'. Although fuelled by tales of the 'Wild West', the creation of the Hollywood film industry and the role of the region as a locus of economic growth, the core components of the dream were originally built upon four principal themes.

- The West represented the promise of opportunity. During much of the nine-teenth century, migration to the Great Plains offered a chance to construct a homestead and become self-reliant. In the 1930s there was an exodus to California from states such as Oklahoma, Kansas, Texas and Colorado where – across large tracts of land – storms, drought and intensive cultivation led to soil erosion and the 'dust bowl'.
- The discovery of gold in 1848 at Sutter's Mill led to the first California Gold Rush. There were later finds of both gold and silver across the West.
- The West – particularly California – has long seemed to represent indepen-dence and a refuge from hardship. Indeed, at times, it has also offered a promise of indulgence: 'The California Dream has been the motivator of health seekers, retirees, entrepreneurs, hedonists, hippies, escapees from Jim Crow or foreign repression, looking (with or without much accurate infor-mation) for a land of opportunity and "the good life"' (Nugent 1999: 5).
- The West also constitutes a form of nostalgia. In certain senses, it is an idea rather than a place. It is identified with the recapturing of a past age and reconnection with both nature and the natural order. As a consequence, in the late nineteenth century, California attracted both health seekers and the builders of utopian colonies.

Some have suggested that the conservative revival of the 1980s, particularly Reaganism, was shaped by some of these notions of the West. Reagan's speeches invoked independence, ambition and the frontier. Furthermore, as his detractors have noted: 'Reagan's imagined "West-as-America" was a retrieval of myths defined by endless reworkings of heroic westerns where simplistic battles were won and stereotyped enemies overcome in the name of right and justice' (Campbell 2000: 87).

All these images should, however, be qualified and placed in context. First, as noted below, the West has become more urban and industrialised. By the end of the twentieth century many western and southwestern cities had begun to absorb the surrounding counties. Although not formally part of the city, they had, Walter Nugent argues, an incipiently metropolitan character. Rural areas, and the industries with which they were traditionally associated, have corre-spondingly been in decline.

> The emptying of farms and small towns, and the disappearing economic signifi-cance of mining and ranching, turned much of the region 180 degrees from what it had been early in the century . . . the West by the end of the 1990s was emphat-ically metropolitan – in its central cities, its suburbs, and its 'incipiently metro-politan' rings. (Nugent 1999: 375)

Second, as some radical critics have noted, the dominant notions of the West are derived from the experience of the white settler moving westward. They rec-ognise that the West was very different for Native Americans and the Latino

population. For these groupings, there is a history of displacement and fragmentation. In practice, the region was – and continues to be – a borderland
within which multiple identities and traditions are situated.

Rustbelt and sunbelt

Economic change – most notably the decline of the 'rustbelt' and the rise of the
'sunbelt' – created new patterns of inter-regional movement across the US. The
term 'rustbelt' became commonplace during the mid-1980s. A description of
northern industrial states such as Illinois, Michigan and Pennsylvania, it captured the process of deindustrialisation and the decline of manufacturing
industries such as steel and automobile production. The US had lost its share of
the world market. Production methods in the rustbelt were often outdated and
productivity levels were relatively low. These industries were uncompetitive
against imports from the Far East. While American industry had stood still, the
Japanese had pioneered new working practices such as just-in-time production.

The decline of the rustbelt had important human consequences. Significant
numbers of communities faced mass unemployment. There was a relative, and
in some cases, absolute decline in population. Labour union membership – formerly concentrated in the 'heavy' industries – fell. Men – who had once thought
that their earnings could support a family – faced a loss of both income and
status. Many, particularly black men, were unable to find alternative employment.

In contrast, there was significant economic expansion and population
growth in the 'sunbelt' states of the South and Southwest. Indeed, between
1970 and 1980, 42 per cent of the total US population increase was concentrated in California, Texas and Florida. There were four principal reasons for
this. Labour costs were lower; the construction of interstate highways allowed
products to be transported over greater distances; the introduction of air con-
ditioning made living and working conditions in the South and Southwest
more acceptable; and a significant number of defence contracts were awarded
to firms located in the sunbelt, leading to wider economic expansion through a
regional multiplier effect. Cities such as Atlanta, Houston, Dallas (Fort Worth)
and Los Angeles grew rapidly.

As Kevin Phillips observed in his 1969 book, *The Emerging Republican
Majority*, the shifting locus of the American economy and population had political consequences. Southerners and westerners were associated with core conservative values such as individualism and traditionalism. The growing
importance of the sunbelt would enable the Republicans to construct a
winning electoral coalition. However, the character and structure of the
sunbelt changed during the 1990s. First, relative rates of economic growth –
in comparison with other sunbelt states – slowed up in Florida and California.
There was also a population shift – predominantly white in character – from

California towards the mountain and desert states. This had consequences for cities such as Denver and Phoenix:

> Rapid development – 'an acre an hour' around Phoenix, whole once-timbered mountainsides east of Seattle, vast pasturelands south of Denver – clashed with ever-louder demands to slow it down. Californian 'equity exiles' drove up real estate prices in the small towns and suburbs they invaded (although the new dollars often revitalized their economies. (Nugent 1999: 369)

Despite immigration, the rate of population growth in California and Florida also slowed up after 1990. There were significantly higher rates of growth in states such as Arizona, Georgia and Florida (*see* Table 7.2). All these states were all awarded increased Congressional representation following the 2000 Census.

Table 7.2   *Population gains and losses, 1990–2000*

State	change %
Arizona	40.0
California	13.8
District of Columbia	−5.7
Florida	23.5
Georgia	26.4
Illinois	8.6
Massachusetts	5.5
New Mexico	20.1
New York	5.5
Pennsylvania	3.4
West Virginia	0.8

Source: Adapted from Nasser 2001:5A.

Although some people moved eastwards because the social problems of the Californian cities, many were lured by the prospect of economic opportunity and an improved quality of life. As William Frey of the Milken Institute noted, the 'new sunbelt' was 'attracting people seeking good jobs and a better quality of life away from crowded freeways and super-priced homes' (quoted in Rosenblatt 2001). Furthermore, as Chapter 6 recorded, whites and significant numbers of African-Americans have been drawn to the southern states during the 1990s. It appeared to represent a more stable and secure way of living.

Migration has had political consequences. The predominantly conservative attitudes of those who left states such as California has reinforced the innate conservatism of the mountain states. At the same time, however, the influx of northerners into the South has diluted the conservatism of the South, strengthening the Democratic Party's prospects in some areas. Businesses also relocated. A number of firms moved from California to neighbouring states because of high income taxes and complex environmental regulations. However, many of those who moved to the new sunbelt were drawn towards the high-tech and service industries that were established in the region. High-technology development accounted for much of the population gain in North Carolina. New automotive plants drew people to Kentucky from outside the state. Biotechnology initiatives at the University of Wisconsin also attracted considerable numbers of 'knowledge workers' from both coasts to Madison.

National identity

Although the process of **globalisation** has led some to portray national identity and loyalty to a flag as an anachronism, there are still strong feelings of patriotism and national loyalty in the US. In June 1994 The Gallup Organization found that 65 per cent of Americans felt 'extremely' or 'very' patriotic, while 28 per cent said they were 'somewhat' patriotic. Only 5 per cent described themselves as 'not especially' patriotic (Crabtree 1999).

Using data from the International Social Survey Program's study of twenty-three nations in 1995, Tom W. Smith and Lars Jarkko drew similar conclusions. They found that 89.9 per cent either 'agreed' or 'agreed strongly' with the statement that they 'would rather be a citizen of the US than of any other country in the world'. This was a higher figure than in any other country. The study also recorded very high levels of pride in the country's specific achievements. 76.5 per cent were 'proud' or 'very proud' of, for example, the American economy, the political system and achievements in science and technology (Smith and Jarkko 1998). Furthermore, there were suggestions – even before the attacks against New York and Washington DC on September 11th 2001 – that national loyalties were becoming more deeply embedded. Although the figure dropped during the mid-1990s, the proportion of eighteen-year-old men registering for the military draft – as required by law – rose back up to 87 per cent in 2000 (*USA Today* 2001).

However, the overall character of American patriotism also encourages a strong sense of loyalty. It has a particular depth and meaning because – in contrast with sentiments in many other countries – it extends beyond ethnic or primordial forms of nationalism that are structured around a sense of affiliation with fellow citizens who share a collective history, cultural traditions or – in some instances – particular racial characteristics. Instead, American nationalism also emphasises the civic character of the US. Although always tempered by racial and ethnic considerations, 'being American' rests upon adherence to ideals such as self-reliance, democracy and a belief in individual freedom. The inculcation of these principles has traditionally been an integral part of the socialisation process in the US, and children begin to identify with both their country and its values at an early age.

Summary

Although some have asserted that economic and political processes have created a centralised nation, regional differences can still be discerned. These were partly bequeathed by the early colonists. However, other factors – most notably mass immigration and the processes of both industrialisation and deindustrialisation – also moulded the contemporary regional structure. In particular, the South has retained a separate identity. New England, the Midwest and West also have distinctive features. The decline of the 'rustbelt', the growth of the 'sunbelt' states, and the shifting character of the sunbelt, have had significant consequences and changed the relationship between the different regions.

References and further reading

Bradshaw, M. (1988), *Regions and Regionalism in the United States*, Basingstoke, Macmillan.

Campbell, N. (2000), *The Cultures of the American New West*, Edinburgh, Edinburgh University Press (BAAS Paperbacks).

Crabtree, S. (1999), *Poll Analyses – Americans Are Widely Patriotic, but Many Think Founding Fathers Would Frown on Modern America*, 2 July, www.gallup.com/Gallup Poll Analyses – Americans Are Widely Patriotic, but Many Think Founding Fathers Would Frown on Modern America.htm

Croly, H. (1989), *The Promise of American Life*, Boston, Northeastern University Press.

Elazar, D. J. (1994), *The American Mosaic: The Impact of Space, Time, and Culture on American Politics*, Boulder, Westview Press.

Escott, P. D. and D. R. Goldfield (eds) (1990), *Major Problems in the History of the American South; Volume 2: The New South*, Lexington, D. C. Heath.

Ezell, J. S. (1988), *The South Since 1865*, Norman, University of Oklahoma Press.

Faragher, J. M. (1999), 'Many wests: place, culture and regional identity', *Pacific Historical Review*, 68:2, February, 108.

Fischer, D. H. (1991), *Albion's Seed: Four British Folkways in America*, New York, Oxford University Press.

Fox-Genovese, E. and E. D. Genovese (2001), 'Surveying the south', *Southern Cultures*, 7:2, Spring, 76.

Gastil, R. D. (1975), *Cultural Regions of the United States*, Seattle, University of Washington Press.

General Social Survey (2001), *1972–2000 Cumulative Datafile*, www.icpsr.umich.edu/G5599/index.html

Genovese, E. D. (1996), *The Southern Tradition: The Achievement and Limitations of an American Conservatism*, Cambridge, MA, Harvard University Press.

Glaser, J. M. (1996), *Race, Campaign Politics, and the Realignment in the South*, New Haven, Yale University Press.

Gray, S. E. (1993), 'The Upper Midwest', *Encyclopedia of American Social History*, Charles Scribner's Sons; reproduced by the History Resource Center, Farmington Hills, Michigan: Gale Group, infotrac.galegroup.com

Heinrich, D. (2001), 'German settlements in the midwest', *Cobblestone*, 22:5, 10.

Hobsbawm, E. J. (1999), *Nations and Nationalism: Programme, Myth, Reality*, Cambridge, Cambridge University Press.

Krakau K. (ed.) (1997), *The American Nation – National Identity – Nationalism*, Munster, Lit Verlag.

Nasser, H. E. (2001), 'Sun belt is still hot, but Census finds a big shift', *USA Today*, 2 January, 5A.

National Park Service (1992), *Lowell: The Story of an Industrial City*, Washington DC, US Department of the Interior.

Nugent, W. (1999), *Into the West: The Story of its People*, New York, Vintage Books.

Phillips, K. P. (1969), *The Emerging Republican Majority*, New Rochelle, Arlington House.

Rosenblatt, R. A. (2001), 'America's bumper crop: all 50 states show population gains', *Los Angeles Times*, 3 April.

Smith, T. W. and L. Jarkko (1998), *National Pride: A Cross-National Analysis*, GSS Cross-National Report 19, Chicago, University of Chicago – National Opinion Research Cente.

Stanley, H. W. and R. G. Niemi (2000), *Vital Statistics on American Politics 1999–2000*, Washington DC, CQ Press.

USA Today (2001), 'Draft registration rises', 5 May.

US Census Bureau (2001), *Historical Income Tables – Households*, www.census.gov/hhes/income/histinc/h06.html

Washington Times (2001), 1 October.

Williams, P. W. (1993), 'New England', *Encyclopedia of American Social History*, Charles Scribner's Sons; reproduced by the History Resource Center, Farmington Hills, Michigan: Gale Group, infotrac.galegroup.com

8

Conclusion:
September 11th and after

The 1990s began amidst fears for the future. A plethora of 'jeremiads' appeared in print, many of which were posed in dramatically apocalyptic terms. Indeed, some foretold the demise of the US itself. However, as the decade progressed, and as this book has charted, many of these anxieties proved to be groundless.

Despite the 1990–91 recession, which denied President George Bush a second term, and fuelled 'outsider' electoral challenges by both Patrick Buchanan and Ross Perot, the 1990s saw the longest period of uninterrupted growth since the 1960s. Although talk of a 'new economy' proved over-optimistic, there was a significant rise in levels of productivity growth. In all, about 24 million jobs were created between January 1991 and January 2001.

There have been recurrent fears that individualism has been displaced by growing conformity. These concerns emerged during the 1950s in David Riesman's book *The Lonely Crowd*, and reappeared in the radical critiques of the American economy and society that were published in the 1980s and 1990s. However, these appraisals of the contemporary US often underestimated the degree to which there have been expressions of dissidence.

Similarly, Robert Putnam's critique, *Bowling Alone* (2000), charting the decline of civic organisations, commanded wide attention. It contributed to a surge in volunteering, a number of long-term projects, and may have contributed to the faith-based charitable initiative that George W. Bush included in his 2000 election platform. However, despite the concerns that underpinned *Bowling Alone*, and fears of hyperindividualism, the long-term picture offers some grounds for encouragement. Indeed, as Claude S. Fischer records, several shifts and changes are increasing Americans' commitment to their localities and neighbourhood organisations. Although still high when compared with the countries of Europe, there is reduced residential mobility. Indeed, for many, there is a renewed sense of attachment to neighbourhood. This is partly because many new neighbourhoods are socially homogeneous. People have something in common with their neighbours because they live together on the basis of income groups. Furthermore, although it levelled off in the 1970s,

149

there is also a high level of home ownership, adding to a feeling of individual investment in a particular area (Fischer 1992: 81–5).

Despite the assertions of those who foresaw moral decline and cultural decay, some traditionalist attitudes began to reassert themselves during the 1990s. Sexual fidelity, for example, seems to have become more highly valued, with a growing emphasis on the stability of relationships and personal responsibility.

Moreover, despite widely shared perceptions, the American region has not been eradicated. There are still – as Chapter 7 recorded – significant differences between areas. In particular, the South has distinct characteristics. While there is considerable geographical mobility, which many have claimed has created a homogeneous national identity, much of this has had a short-range character. In many instances it involves movement between only the core of the metropolitan region and the hinterland (Elazar 1994: 291). In a survey that supplemented the 2000 Census, 67 per cent of native-born Americans say they are still living in their state of birth. Even in California – the state most closely associated with population shifts, 68.3 per cent of US native residents were born within the state. At 82.4 per cent, New York had the highest proportion of nonmovers.

Nonetheless, the US was not unchanged at the end of the 1990s. First, despite the resurgence in moral traditionalism, there was a shift in attitudes towards sex and sexuality. As Chapter 5 recorded, some liberal attitudes became increasingly institutionalised, at least within the metropolitan regions. Premarital sexual activity has become a norm and there is greater acceptance, although not approval, of homosexuality. There are, therefore, cultural contradictions that have created a form of political stalemate. Against this background, when faced by shifting beliefs and competing definitions of moral conduct, legislators may well fear to tread.

Second, the character and consequences of long-term demographic shifts began to become evident. Chapter 6 charted the growing gulf between the metropolitan regions around the edges of the US – which have a multi-ethnic and multicultural character – and the predominantly white 'heartlands'. Increasingly, this cleavage cuts across the traditional regions and may yet supercede the long-established divide between the 'Yankee' and those from the South, West And Midwest. The consequences of the divide were evident in the 2000 presidential election. The country was polarised between those metropolitan regions that had a multi-ethnic character – along the eastern and western seaboards and around the Great Lakes – which backed Al Gore, the Democrats' candidate – and the predominantly white 'heartlands'. In this sense, there is a degree of political 'Balkanisation'.

Third, there was – as the decade progressed – a growing sense of optimism. Surveys suggest that the mood was widely shared, except among some in the 18–29 age cohort (Morin 1998). The prevailing mood boosted the 'futurology' industry and led to predictions of further change. Although there were fears of a 'digital divide' between those who had access to new technology and low-income groups who were excluded, many observers spoke, for example, of the possibilities unleashed by the internet. Some argued that the absence of a formal structure of ownership and control would lead to a culture based upon sharing and co-operation. In such circumstances, governments and corporations could no longer maintain a climate of secrecy. Notions of free speech would be reinvigorated. There would be accelerated progress towards a globalised economy in which frontiers were increasingly irrelevant. Discrimination would be lessened. In an era of online communication and commerce, an individual's sex, race or ethnicity is – even if known – of little consequence.

Other developments, it was said, were also encouraging fundamental social change. Reduced product development times and the need to minimise costs require a pooling of knowledge. There will be a need for greater flexibility. Much more will therefore be leased rather than purchased, and firms will only maintain a minimal infrastructure. Furthermore, vertical, 'top-down' structures will have to be dismantled. Hierarchies are unimaginative and unresponsive. Indeed, the concept of the independent company has had its day: 'The old idea of autonomous, boundaried business enterprises is giving way to the notion of multiple partners embedded deep in one another's operations and engaged in both formal and informal reciprocal relationships' (Rifkin 2000: 45)

This shift in the character of economic activity is reflected in philosophical change. Whereas modernist philosophies emphasised certainty, laws of development and the application of science, postmodernism stresses that there is no knowable reality. Instead, there is contingency, embeddedness and diversity. Furthermore, people live for the present. The dividing lines between 'reality' and the imagination are becoming more fluid and indeterminate. Jean Baudrillard's celebrated assertion that television was the 'real' world has some credibility in an age when, as a 1999 survey reported, American children spent five and a half hours a day watching television (Rifkin 2000: 196).

The emphasis upon change and unbounded possibilities – which were intertwined with an overall sense of optimism – reshaped the American understanding of the world. In 1989, as the Cold War came to a close, *The National Interest* published an influential article by Francis Fukuyama (1989). Although widely misinterpreted, 'The end of history?' was an attempt to turn Marxism on its head. In its crude or 'vulgar' form, Marxism had depicted communism as the final stage of human development that followed the feudal, capitalist and socialist orders. The intense class conflict that had characterised these early stages would come to an end. The character of the economic, social and political order would be settled for all time. In that sense, history would come to an end.

For Fukuyama, the free market economy was the final stage of human development. With the collapse of the Soviet bloc, and China's incorporation into the world market, conflicts about the character of society, the economy and the proper role of government were being settled. History was coming to an end as the world moved inexorably towards deregulated market economies and the adoption of liberal democracy. International commerce was washing away past ideologies, tribal prejudices and localist anxieties. Conflicts within nations and battles between nations would eventually – in the language of Marxism – 'wither away'. During the decade that followed 'The end of history?' Fukuyama's ideas were popularised. They contributed, in particular, to the claim that no two nations within which a branch of Macdonald's has been opened go to war with each other. Although the wars in the former Yugoslavia and NATO's bombing of Belgrade refuted the literal truth of the proposition, the equation between free market economics and international co-operation – which reflected the ingrained optimism of the period – remained influential.

The attacks

Much has been said about the attacks on the twin towers of the World Trade Center and the Pentagon on September 11th 2001. The terrorists struck at the heart of the country's commercial and political institutions and about 3,000 civilians met their deaths. There was a profound sense of violation, particularly because the mainland US had been spared from attack during the First and Second World Wars. In economic terms, the loss was between $25 billion and $60 billion (Becker and Murphy 2001).

Although some of the consequences – most notably the degree of political consensus, and the extent to which Americans rallied around George W. Bush's presidency – may prove short-term, the attacks initially appeared to have led to some significant long-term changes. They remoulded the popular mood in profound ways. For example, the sense of optimism – that had characterised the latter half of the 1990s – was displaced by feelings of anxiety and uncertainty. This was reflected in measures of consumer confidence which – already slipping before September 11th – dived down. Many of the hopes and promises of a new economy, which had dominated the latter half of the 1990s, also came to a close. While there were different estimates of the recession's depth and length, claims that the business cycle – the process of boom and slump – had been finally eliminated, disappeared. Furthermore, supply-side economics – which asserted that the prospects for growth depended on measures such as marginal tax rate reductions that would release entrepreneurial skills and create a more flexible labour market – lost ground among economists and policy makers. Growing numbers instead called for the boosting of consumer demand through a fiscal stimulus package.

Furthermore, the religious right – whose critique of family decline was discussed in Chapter 5 – and those associated with the far Right, lost some of their former influence. There were signs of this during the latter half of the 1990s, particularly in the impeachment crisis, when, to the chagrin of many conservatives, public opinion seemed indifferent to President Clinton's actions. The weakened position of the religious Right became evident beyond doubt, however, in the aftermath of September 11th. Pat Robertson of the Christian Coalition and Jerry Falwell, who led the Moral Majority during the 1980s, asserted that the attacks had been caused because God had – faced by the mass immorality of the American people – lifted his protection from the US. Their remarks were immediately disowned by the White House.

There has also been a change in the character of public intellectual discourse. Fukuyama's vision of a world market economy – based upon the progressive dissipation of past prejudices – lost credence in the wake of September 11th. Instead, other theorists commanded increased respect. Samuel Huntington's book, *The Clash of Civilizations*, attracted particular attention. He argues that the world is divided into six or seven large-scale blocs and the US faces challenges by the Islamic nations and China. This requires, Huntington argues, a much more confident assertion of western values. The US cannot assume that the market will simply dissolve past prejudices. Instead, it should become much more of a missionary nation.

Benjamin Barber's book, *Jihad vs. McWorld* (1996), also proved influential (see Chapter 4). While Huntington is associated with the neo-conservative Right, Barber offers a radical analysis. He points to the emergence and growth of 'McWorld'. In most countries, the last vestiges of civil society – such as voluntary and civic organisations – have been lost as the logic of commercialism extended itself. Everything – including production, consumption, distribution and leisure – is being subordinated to the soulless pursuit of profit, leaving little room for imagination and creativity. Identity politics are a response to McWorld. They incorporate nationalism and, in its most vehement form, *Jihad*, the struggle of believers against faithlessness and the faithless.

For much of the 1990s, popular opinion had a **unilateralist** edge. Many felt that the US should not become embroiled abroad, and should consider its national and strategic interests alone. Such sentiments seemed to underpin the actions of the Bush administration during its early months in office. In the aftermath of the attacks, increasing numbers began to think in cautiously **multilateralist** terms, although many felt that international co-operation should be organised on US terms. The Pew Research Center found that while only 38 per cent wanted to see the US again take the lead in world affairs in early September 2001, the proportion had risen to 48 per cent by late October. Similarly, the numbers believing that the US should take its allies' views into account rose from 45 to 59 per cent during the same period (The Pew Research Center for the People and the Press 2001).

There was a further and, perhaps in the long term, more significant shift. American popular thinking has – as this book has argued – been structured around a tension between individualism and the ties that bind individuals to families, communities and the nation. September 11th appears to have brought about a shift towards the latter. There was, for example, a surge in volunteering.

One organisation, Hands On Atlanta, reported that the numbers offering to help others jumped from 500 to nearly a 1,000 a month. Similarly, VolunteerMatch.org, a non-profit website that links volunteers with agencies, went from an average of 20,000 visits a month to 36,000. Enquiries to the Points of Light Foundation, a network with 500 centres across the country, saw an 80 per cent increase (Copeland 2001). As Andrew Sullivan records this went together with a cultural shift. There was, he argues, a new humility among the upper and upper-middle class who had, during the 1980s and 1990s, been associated with both conspicuous consumption and the pursuit of narrow self-interest. In the wake of the attacks, there was, in place of this, a celebration of manual workers (Sullivan 2001).

There was also a renewed sense of national pride. Furthermore, although the proportion expressing trust in the institutions of government was lower than in the late 1950s and 1960s – when statistics were first collected – the degree of trust was significantly higher than at any time in the 1990s (see Table 8.1). Although those questioned by pollsters may simply have been responding to the exigencies of the crisis, some observers suggested that these renewed feelings of trust might lay the basis for greater government activism and a shift away from the anti-government sentiments that had shaped politics during the preceding decades.

Table 8.1   *Trust in government, 1990–2001*

How much of the time do you think you can trust government in Washington to do what is right – just about always, most of the time, or only some of the time? (Answers in percentages.)

	Just about always	Most of the time	Only some of the time	Never	No opinion
(Oct.) 2001	13	47	38	1	1
2000	4	40	55	1	1
1998	4	36	58	1	1
1996	3	30	66	1	0
1994	2	19	74	3	0
1992	3	26	68	2	1
1990	3	25	68	2	2

Source: Adapted from The Gallup Organization 2001.

Survey evidence suggests that feelings of trust and patriotic pride extended across the demographic divide. They were shared, for example, by African-Americans. As T. D. Jakes, a black television evangelist told a predominantly black congregation in Dallas: 'This wasn't my country when I got here. But it is now. Too much blood was spilt. If slavery didn't run us out, if Jim Crow didn't run us out, if the Depression didn't run us out, if war didn't run us out . . . no terrorist group is going to run us out!' (Quoted in Cannon 2001: 3061).

Feelings such as these may be eroded with the passage of time, or if the administration is unable to meet the popular expectations that have been aroused. Few would doubt, however, that American society and identity are in a state of flux.

References and further reading

Barber, B. R. (1996), *Jihad vs. McWorld: How Globalism and Tribalism are Reshaping the World*, New York, Ballantine Books.

Becker, G. S. and K. M. Murphy (2001), 'Prosperity will rise out of the ashes', *The Wall Street Journal*, 29 October.

Cannon, C. M. (2001), Between fear and faith, *National Journal*, 6 October, 3058–62.

Copeland, L. (2001), 'More volunteer since Sept. 11', *USA Today*, 23 November.

Elazar, D. J. (1994), *The American Mosaic: The Impact of Space, Time, and Culture on American Politics*, Boulder, Westview Press.

Fischer, C. S. (1992), 'Ambivalent communities: how Americans understand their localities', in A. Wolfe (ed.), *America at Century's End*, Berkeley, University of California Press.

Fukuyama, F. (1989), 'The end of history?', *The National Interest*, 16, Summer, 3–18.

The Gallup Organization (2001), *Poll Analyses – Trust in Government Increases Sharply in Wake of Terrorist Attacks*, 12 October, www.gallup.com/Gallup Poll Analyses – Trust in Government Increases Sharply In Wake of Terrorist Attacks.htm

Huntington, S. P. (1998), *The Clash of Civilizations and the Remaking of World Order*, London, Touchstone Books.

Morin, R. (1998), 'Nobody's happy', *The Washington Post*, 31 August, washington-post.com/wp-srv/politics/polls/wat/archive/wat083198.htm

The Pew Research Center for the People and the Press (2001), *America's New Internationalist Point of View*, 24 October, www.people-press.org/reports/display.php3?ReportID=141

Putnam, R. D. (2000), *Bowling Alone: The Collapse and Revival of American Community*, New York, Simon & Schuster.

Riesman, D. (1962), *The Lonely Crowd: A Study of the Changing American Character*, New Haven, Yale University Press.

Rifkin, J. (2000), *The Age of Access: The New Culture of Hypercapitalism, Where all of Life is a Paid-For Experience*, New York, Jeremy P. Tarcher.

Sullivan, A. (2001), 'How the firemen shifted America's culture', *Sunday Times*, 2 December.

Index

157